TEACHING MEDIA LITERACY

A How-To-Do-It Manual® and CD-ROM

Belinha S. De Abreu

HOW-TO-DO-IT MANUALS FOR LIBRARIANS

NUMBER 156

NEAL-SCHUMAN PUBLISHERS, INC.

New York   London

To my parents, Jose and Francelina De Abreu, who have always believed in the power of education and its value in our lives—com muito amor, BDA.

Published by Neal-Schuman Publishers, Inc.
100 William St., Suite 2004
New York, NY 10038

Library of Congress Cataloging-in-Publication Data

ISBN-13: 978-1-55570-596-1
ISBN-10: 1-55570-596-0

De Abreu, Belinha S.
    Teaching media literacy : a how-to-do-it manual and CD-ROM / Belinha S. De Abreu.
        p. cm.—(How-to-do-it manuals for librarians ; no. 156)
    Includes bibliographical references and index.
    ISBN-13: 978-1-55570-596-1
    ISBN-10: 1-55570-596-0
    1. Media literacy—Study and teaching.   I. Title.
P96.M4D4 2007
302.23071—dc22   2007007784

CONTENTS

LIST OF FIGURES

FOREWORD

Media literacy is starting to attract attention. State standards and education courses address its importance. Educators discuss it at national conferences and summer institutes. New classroom resources support the integration of media literacy into the curriculum. These accomplishments are all good news for those teachers who are already eager to accommodate their students' interest in popular culture. Other teachers may have reservations about bringing controversial topics into the classroom or may feel unprepared without an organized curriculum.

Teaching Media Literacy combats those reservations with its combination of theory and practice. Teachers, especially those reluctant to teach media literacy, need a practical guide like this one. Belinha De Abreu's lesson plans address both analysis and production, providing the building blocks of an authentic media education.

Teaching Media Literacy also helps educators pinpoint important teachable moments, from the coverage of September 11 and Hurricane Katrina to the Academy Awards or a new video game. Each lesson includes objectives, materials, assessments, and reflection. De Abreu provides challenging key questions and multimedia tie-ins to launch follow-up activities. In the comprehensive resources section, teachers will find the best Web sites, listservs, films, books, periodicals, and media education organizations, all of which can help make lessons more vibrant and relevant.

De Abreu's in-depth explorations of cultural contexts and media conventions make media study more meaningful. I feel sure that the clear path through the media environment outlined in these pages will inspire other educators in their own media literacy journeys.

Barry Duncan
Media Education Consultant
Author of *Mass Media and Popular Culture*

PREFACE

"No matter what the source, information is only powerful if students know what to do with it. As students are inundated with media messages, the challenge is not to amass more information, but to access, organize, and evaluate useful information from a variety of print and electronic sources."

—*Kathleen Tyner, author of* Literacy in a Digital World

Look around a teenager's bedroom and you will see what shapes his or her world: print media, television, the Internet, radio, music CDs, iPods, DVDs, and video games. With all these different (and often competing) streams of information, media literacy, the ability to critically evaluate, analyze, and create media messages, is increasingly necessary for survival.

Media producers do their best to captivate consumers. For example, television programming has to be compelling to avoid cancellation: images, speed, and content are all conscientiously designed to mesmerize specific demographic groups. Impressionable teenagers have always been a desirable demographic. The media increasingly target younger children as well. Children and teenagers, though easily influenced, have the least control over the messages they receive. Additionally, peer pressure may lead them to imitate their friends' preferences. Unfortunately, what they learn from the media is not always accurate, reliable, or fair.

Today's educators have an obligation to help students understand the media-saturated world. Media literacy education encourages students to examine media messages critically rather than accepting them at face value. This topic should certainly have a place in our schools. But where does media literacy fit in our already overloaded school curriculum? Almost anywhere! For school library specialists, media literacy provides a new way to teach higher-order critical thinking skills. Classroom teachers can enhance students' comprehension of core subject areas by using media tie-ins. Any educator can use the media, which students already know and value, to create dynamic lessons and opportunities for learning. *Teaching Media Literacy: A How-To-Do-It Manual* gives school library specialists, teachers, and curriculum advisors new instructional tools to help them in this endeavor.

Some educators still shy away from media topics. At a recent conference at MIT, this matter dominated a seminar attended by Boston-area teachers. Audience members said they were afraid of giving their opinion or afraid of parental or administrative disapproval, but ultimately they feared that they, as educators, were not as knowledgeable about the media as their students were. This fear, while common, is unnecessary. Effective media literacy instruction depends on the teaching of principles, not only on specific media texts. You may not be familiar with the latest music, but you can still use the artists your students love to lead an educational and enlightening lesson on music video censorship.

The effectiveness of media study sometimes surprises both teachers and students. Teachers find it easy to integrate media into their subject areas. Students enjoy discussing and evaluating some of their favorite topics. When students realize the teacher is not going to pass judgment on their choices, they become eager to share their likes and dislikes. Media literacy instruction is a way to use real-world topics in the classroom while giving students skills that will remain with them for a lifetime.

ORGANIZATION

This book is divided into three parts. Part I, "Media Literacy and the Curriculum," examines the theory behind the topic and its significance to librarians, teachers, and students.

Chapter 1, "Defining Media Literacy," explains the general parameters upon which the lessons in Part II are based. It also gives examples of how national organizations use the term and answers questions readers may have.

Chapter 2, "Understanding the Significance of Media Literacy for Students," discusses how the media attract the attention of children and influence their consumer choices and their personal lives.

Chapter 3, "Adding Media Literacy into the Curriculum," reveals the current state of students' media knowledge and emphasizes the importance of teaching this topic.

Chapter 4, "Providing Media Literacy in the School Library and Content Area Classrooms," shows creative ways to integrate media literacy into standard subject areas. Readers will learn how to successfully teach media literacy both independently and as part of a collaborative team.

Part II, "Ready-to-Teach Lessons," demonstrates lesson development and provides actual lessons used with students. Each chapter includes adaptations to different grade levels and the URLs of related Web sites.

Chapter 5, "Television," incorporates analysis of newscasts, a discussion of reality TV, and a look at how sitcoms and dramas reflect, or more often don't reflect, real life.

Chapter 6, "Movies," highlights ways to use movies in the classroom environment. In these lessons, students will investigate how movies influence society and compare historical films with the historical events they represent.

Chapter 7, "Photography and Images," addresses photo manipulation and the value of the photograph. The lessons in this chapter teach students about photo appreciation and interpretation.

Chapter 8, "Music and Radio," includes lessons covering musical genres, the messages in music videos, the importance of radio play, and issues of censorship.

Chapter 9, "Advertising," deconstructs media images and the unique language used by marketers to reveal the truth behind commercial messages. These lessons will help the reader teach students to be critical consumers and knowledgeable buyers.

Chapter 10, "Media Production and Other Digital Technologies," discusses the importance of students' participation in the creation of their own original projects. Production lessons give students an opportunity to demonstrate what they think of media messages while gaining hands-on real-world experience.

Chapter 11, "Emerging Educational Technologies: The Future Is Now," explains how to use new technologies such as MP3s, iPods, and Web applications in the classrooms of today and the future.

Each chapter is followed by supplemental sections describing various extended activities and including activity sheets.

Part III, "Teaching Media Literacy: The Resources," includes a glossary of terms, as well as lists of Web sites, videos, fiction and nonfiction books, media literacy organizations, and other resources.

The accompanying CD-ROM includes copies of all student handouts and worksheets for easy reproduction.

Media literacy lessons are increasingly important to growth and development. Students receive countless media messages every day, and media moguls are always finding new ways to sell their products to youth. There is no stopping these influences. Our role is to create an environment in which free and open discussion can take place. If we teach media literacy well, students will become independent and thoughtful media consumers.

ACKNOWLEDGMENTS

When writing a book there are always many people to thank, from those who inspired to those who provided different ideas, those who taught you, and those who helped you through the process. Without all of their help, this book would not be possible:

My students at the Walsh Intermediate School in Branford, Connecticut, who taught me much about the importance of their media choices. You are the ones who made this book possible.

My hometown editor and friend, Michele Simpson, who helped me to write, rewrite, and write again. If it weren't for your help and guidance, this book would have not been as well organized. You allowed me to write freely without worries of the red pen. Thank you also for allowing some of these lessons to be tested in your very classroom. You have my sincere gratitude.

My teachers in the world of media literacy: David Considine, Barry Duncan, David Buckingham, Kathleen Tyner, and Diane Samples. Your voices have all guided me in the instruction of media literacy. I am grateful for all that I have learned from each of you.

My friends in the world of media literacy, but especially Nicki Soice and Maggie Annerino, who helped me to see the possibilities of many of these lessons. You provided endless encouragement.

My editors at Neal-Schuman: Miguel Figueroa, Michael Kelley, and Elizabeth Lund. Thank you for keeping me on task throughout the writing process.

My sister, Grace De Abreu Small, who pushed me to finish and even took some of these lessons to her own classroom.

Lastly and most importantly, my husband, Jay Lindberg, who has always believed in and supported my work. My love and thanks.

MEDIA LITERACY AND THE CURRICULUM

1 DEFINING MEDIA LITERACY

"Media literacy courses can give young people the power to recognize the difference between entertainment, television that is just bad and the information they need to make good decisions. What they need is a clear awareness of how the media influences, shapes and defines their lives."
—*Richard Riley, U.S. Secretary of Education, December 13, 1995*

Do the media ask us to live by certain prescribed rules? Are we predisposed to certain attitudes by how ideas and pictures are presented to us in various media? From the moment radio was introduced into our living rooms and when the first picture box was delivered, the media have influenced our lives increasingly.

The media have brought us some of the most amazing stories of our times. They have become both a learning instrument and an idea producer. However, they have also become a source of mixed messages that are both negative and positive influences on our youth. What do we as educators need to teach about questioning television's messages? Where in education does media literacy fit in our already overbooked school curriculum? How does the library media specialist help to integrate this literacy with subject areas, thereby fostering new relationships with classroom educators?

Media literacy is vital to the growth of our students' perception of the world around them. Consider the following statistics:

- Television viewing is the number-one after-school activity for six- to seventeen-year-olds (Kaiser Family Foundation, 2005).

- In the average American home with children, the TV is on nearly sixty hours a week (Nielsen Survey, 2005).

- The average child sees 20,000 TV commercials every year (American Academy of Pediatrics, 1995).

- Only about 20 percent of all characters on children's television are female (Kaiser Family Foundation, 2005).

- Internet consumption is, predictably, increasing faster than any other category of media (Foundations of Library and Information Science, 2004).

These five statistics alone suggest that the media have dominated the lives of today's children. Today's children learn more from what they see on television than they do in the classroom.

Consistently, media messages are integral in the growth and learning of today's youth. Consider this cartoon set out by the author of Calvin and Hobbes (Figure 1-1).

Figure 1-1. "Cardboard TV Screen" by Bill Watterson
(**CALVIN AND HOBBES** © 1990 Watterson. Dist. By Universal Press
Syndicate. Reprinted with permission. All rights reserved.)

The statement is obvious: Television is readily turned on and the messages are not always wanted, but they are forced upon all of us regularly. Children have less say about what those messages are than others, because they have not learned how to control their own environments. They are, in many cases, the sponges of learning that we most desire in school but that we must be very cautious toward while mixing them in with the real world.

Media literacy is an opportunity for learning that provides the openness by which student and teacher can converse and respectfully give divergent opinions. The media give us those teachable moments that illustrate some of the more crucial topics we want students to learn such as character, dedication, honesty, and more. As this piece is being written, the *New York Times* reporter Judith Miller has been released from prison after refusing to reveal who her source was that revealed the name of a CIA operative. This one incident provided many lessons in my classroom on censorship, the trustworthiness of the news industry, and discernment on journalistic practices and certainly a look at our political system. Ultimately the classroom became a place by which students could lend their voice to the conversations that were taking place nationally. This is a teachable moment, and many more of them are afforded to us regularly by the media. Many of these media moments tie in nicely with the science, math, language arts, or social studies curriculum.

Media literacy lessons are central to the growth and development of this generation and future generations of students. Without teaching these vital lessons, we stand to have future citizens who are unsavvy and unwilling to question the thinking behind media messages. So let's begin the process by understanding what it all means.

WHAT IS MEDIA LITERACY?

What is media literacy? This question has been asked in several academic circles. Most of the time, media literacy is grouped with critical thinking and critical literacy. Some academics suggest that it is an extension of other literacies such as reading and writing, except that the text looks different. Many in the area of library science would consider media literacy a part of information literacy, yet that is not quite right either. In order to better understand the definition, it is best to break it down and define each part.

Let's begin with the first part of the term: media. Media consist of newspapers, magazines, cinema films, radio, television, photographs, the World Wide Web, billboards, books, CDs, DVDs, videocassettes, advertisements, and computer games. The growth of media formats is in a constant state of flux. There were once only a few media formats, such as television and radio. Now, media messages are even transmitted via iPods and mobile phones.

Literacy in its most basic form is defined as the ability to read and write. This form of literacy is fundamental to the growth of students in preparing them to understand the world around them. Combining the two terms, media literacy becomes a bridge that reveals that the way students read the world has changed very much in recent years. Media literacy requires that we look beyond printed text and validate the ways in which media play a huge role in our students' lives.

Art Silverblatt, professor of Communications and Journalism at Webster University in St. Louis, Missouri, provides one of the most comprehensive definitions of media literacy:

> Media literacy emphasizes the following elements: a critical thinking skill that allows audiences to develop independent judgments about media content; an understanding of the process of mass communication; an awareness of the impact of media on the individual and society; the development of strategies with which to discuss and analyze media messages; an awareness of media content as "text" that provides insight into our contemporary culture and ourselves; the cultivation of an enhanced enjoyment, understanding, and appreciation of media content; and in the case of media communicator, the ability to produce effective and responsible media messages. (Silverblatt 2001, 120)

While this definition may seem complex, it expresses just four basic tenets. Media literacy is the ability to access, analyze, evaluate, and communicate information in a variety of forms and formats. These terms are ones that most educators will recognize as being a part of Bloom's Taxonomy, which promotes the concept of critical thinking at its highest level. Media literacy promotes critical thinking beyond its traditional forms. It also includes visual and computer literacies.

James Potter in his textbook *Media Literacy* explains that these literacies are key components in the definition of media literacy.

> Media literacy is a set of perspectives that we actively use to expose ourselves to the media to interpret the meaning of the messages we encounter. We build our perspectives from knowledge structures. To build our structures, we need tools and raw materials. These tools are our skills. The raw materials are information from the media and from the real world. Active use means that we are aware of the messages and consciously interacting with them. (Potter 2005, 22)

In essence, media literacy is a continuum that does not stop once the skills are learned. Individuals continue to build upon their literacy as they participate in the media experience. In most cases, no two people will experience the same media environment in exactly the same way. Therefore, media literacy cannot be based on one interpretation of media messages. We must accept differences and divergent thoughts in order to foster analysis and evaluation.

The Partnership for 21st Century Skills, an advocacy organization made up of business leaders, educators, and policymakers, have tried to define what a future citizen in the twenty-first century will need to have in order to work in our global society. They have proposed that the study of media, visual, and information literacy must be included in school curriculums nationally.

One of the greatest benefits of teaching media literacy is giving a voice to the student. Other forms of literacy also give students a voice, but that voice is more obvious in the area of media literacy because the "message" is a vitally important piece of students' lives. Students can provide a more personal perspective on how the media have been a part of their consciousness. A discourse in media can potentially be a transformative supplement to traditional literacies. One very familiar example is tying literature to a film or television adaptation. Visual literacy connects to studies of film, television, photography, and music videos. Our willingness to foster such connections demonstrates an important change in the current educational paradigm.

THE FIVE CORE CONCEPTS AND QUESTIONS

In media literacy circles across the country, the standard by which media literacy skills are taught are based on the five core concepts and five core questions adapted from the Ministry of Ontario, *Media Literacy Resource Guide*, written by the Association for Media Literacy in Toronto, Canada, and later modified by media literacy educators at the Center for Media Literacy in Los Angeles, California.

1. All media messages are "constructed." Who creates the message?

    The first step in teaching media literacy is showing students simply that media messages exist. Understanding "who" is putting the message forth is the other piece of the puzzle, and the more useful part. Media messages are placed in the public sphere with an idea in mind. Marketers spend time collecting data and interpreting messages so that they can immediately know how to construct a message to appeal to a particular audience. Many media messages are based on market research that investigates the effects of different types of images on the consumer. Words and colors are not just selected at random. For instance, marketers use certain colors to appeal to certain cultural communities. Advertisements are placed in certain magazines with an idea of who the audience is and how the reader will perceive the message. For example, ads for glamorous hotels will not be designed in bright orange, greens, or reds; instead, muted colors of beige, black, and white are used. Usually those ads will also include people who would fit the image or the concept of the product. The people shown in ads are often stereotypes. On the opposite end of the spectrum, fast-food ads often incorporate bright colors and bold design to stimulate the appetite for their food.

2. Media messages are constructed using a creative language with its own rules. What techniques are used to attract my attention?

    This creative language is not so much "creative" as targeted to a specific audience. In order to understand the message, students must analyze and deconstruct the message from start to finish. For example, brightly colored letters usually mean children are the intended audience. Words popping out of an advertisement are trying to reach a different audience. The fonts used for medication ads are more severe, which seems to emphasize the seriousness of the issue.

    Television shows are developed with a certain constructed language as well. Programs that have a comedic intent tend to begin with fonts and words that roll or move quickly in a way that seems to emulate laughter. Horror movies have music that leads us to an understanding that a dramatic or frightening event is about to

The Five Core Concepts

- All media messages are "constructed."
- Media messages are constructed using a creative language with its own rules.
- Different people experience the same media message differently.
- Media have embedded values and points of view.
- Media messages are constructed to gain profit and/or power.

The Five Core Questions

- Who creates the message?
- What techniques are used to attract my attention?
- How might different people understand this message differently from me?
- What lifestyles, values, and points of view are represented in or omitted from this message?
- Why was this message sent?

occur. Television dramas are written in ways that make the plots intricate, with three or four stories going on simultaneously within the one drama. The script is fast paced and the actors are directed to speak in that way, with quirky and complex language which in turn makes viewers see the television show as more intelligent. The list goes on. Though constructed messages like these reach us every day, schools do not usually teach students to recognize them. The language of media is just as important as the language of literature. The meaning derived from the text, not the medium, is what makes a text valuable or invaluable.

3. Different people experience the same media message differently. How might different people understand this message differently from me?

While this may seem like an obvious statement, children and young teens are not always aware that another perspective exists. Their thinking has been heavily influenced by their communities, family backgrounds, racial backgrounds, and peer groups. Their perspective is limited. Because of this, it is easy to see how children will believe what they see on television as truth and believe it without question. Asking students to consider what someone in a poor neighborhood or a rich neighborhood would think about a product or a television program, or asking if what they are seeing is "real," can foster a provoking conversation. Asking questions such as these gets students thinking about different perspectives. They might start to understand why someone who is Hispanic may be offended by a Taco Bell ad or why a black family would not find a program that has only white characters as endearing or entertaining. Analyzing music and the news while keeping in mind that not all media representations are accurate creates invaluable lessons. The discussion can be extended to stereotypes in the contexts of movies, music videos, and television programs. Promote higher-order thinking skills by examining how the mainstream media subscribe to those stereotypes in order for the audience to recognize the story, plot, and theme. Many, many lessons can be derived from these basic themes.

4. Media have embedded values and points of view. What lifestyles, values, and points of view are represented in or omitted from this message?

This concept is most significant to parents. Parents usually want to pass on their own values to their children. Often, their values and beliefs are not the same as those transmitted by the media. They may fear that the media have more influence over their children than they do. In schools, teachers have a unique opportunity to discuss and deconstruct the media's values and messages. When students recognize that media have values and points of view, this naturally leads them to realize that there are many points of view on any one topic. Whether teachers are discussing political messages or even a basic television advertisement, students have an opportunity to understand the audience and the ideas behind the message. Most importantly, the discussion of who is omitted from media messages must also be a part of the discussion of any media literacy curriculum. News stories in magazines, the evening news, and newspapers prove time and time again that there is a bias and general underrepresentation of certain racial groups. It is more common to see a criminal represented as black than white. Many criminals themselves understand the media's bias and use it to their advantage when they are being investigated for a crime.

One of the most horrific crimes of recent times serves as an example. Andrea Yates, after drowning her five children, released statements to the press and to the police indicating that a dark man, possibly black or Hispanic, had kidnapped her children. Yates hoped that the police and the media would immediately believe her description because it fit common stereotypes. As we later learned, she had harmed her own children. These types of incidents happen regularly. The media have become a part of the problem of how people are represented.

The media can also reinforce gender-based stereotypes. Magazines that show photographs of models who are incredibly thin or photographs that have been radically airbrushed demonstrate a point of view that is not accurate and certainly not based on how an average American woman looks or feels.

Many contemporary issues can be studied using the media. Basing lessons on vital issues like these has valuable implications for the classroom.

5. Media messages are constructed to gain profit and/or power. Why was this message sent?

   Money is a key reason why media messages exist. Even when car commercials show wonderful new safety gimmicks, their ultimate motive is to convince us, the buyers, to purchase the vehicle at a high cost. Each medium produces messages that are driven by profit motives. The cost of the product includes a portion of the price of advertising. Very few students are aware of this fact. Lessons can be shaped around showing students how the cost of goods is inflated by advertising, testing the claims made about advertised products, or even simply demonstrating the overwhelming presence of advertising in their lives. Some students do not even consider that the brand names visible on their clothing are a form of advertising.

The best part of this concept is that talking about money in relation to goods can be very entertaining for students. Lessons in this area can often be done in conjunction with math and science teachers. For example, teachers can conduct a taste test of a soft drink or test a product to verify that the information provided is accurate. One activity that is done in many middle school science classrooms is to test the pH balance of shampoos and compare them with the advertisements, while reflecting on the cost of the product. This is a chemistry lesson that has been extended to become a media literacy lesson with the purpose of considering product, profit, and truth in advertising.

THE PURPOSE OF TEACHING MEDIA LITERACY

Each of these core concepts and core questions requires higher order thinking, which is many times associated with critical thinking. Analysis and evaluation are the fundamental thought processes necessary for media literacy. In the case of media literacy, "analysis" is about deconstructing messages, detecting bias, and propaganda but also involves the skills of detecting the construction of a wide range of media messages, as well as how they construct reality for the viewer. A variety of lessons will show how this can be done effectively in the classroom.

As the cartoon in Figure 1-2 suggests, media literacy may mean that we require students to think a little more about their media choices. It is really not meant to ruin their entertainment value; although you will have some students who will claim you are trying to ruin their entertainment sources, this is, of course, not the intent of media literacy education. What is most important is to understand that media are a valuable commodity to this generation of students. This will be discussed further in Chapter 2, but it is important to emphasize because there are some very real concrete facts about what media literacy is not. Media literacy educators from various universities across the United States and Canada came up with a list of unsuitable media practices in the classroom:

- "Media bashing" is NOT media literacy; however, media literacy sometimes involves criticizing the media.

- Merely producing media is NOT media literacy, although media literacy should include media production.

- Just teaching with videos or CD-ROMs or other mediated content is NOT media literacy; one must also teach about media.

- Simply looking for political agendas, stereotypes, or misrepresentations is NOT media literacy; there should also be an exploration of the systems making those representations appear "normal."

- Looking at a media message or a mediated experience from just one perspective is NOT media literacy, because media should be examined from multiple positions.

- Media literacy does NOT mean "don't watch"; it means "watch carefully, think critically." (Share 2002, 21)

Literacy in the twenty-first century will require a pedagogical change. The current education system has for a long time promoted very little discourse and has made even fewer accommodations for new literacies. Since birth, this generation of students has been bombarded by media messages and new forms of technology. Indeed, they are the most media-saturated generation that has ever lived. They are active viewers and engagers of all popular culture texts in all its formats. They are known as Generation Y or the Millennials. This generation is defined by being born between 1980 and 1999. They were born into a world where they have used many forms of technology from

Figure 1-2. "Critical Viewer" by John P. Wood
(Used with permission.)

an early age: the Internet, especially the World Wide Web and Instant Messaging; PCs with operating systems that require fewer keystrokes; video games; cellular phones; DVDs; digital music forms such as the MP3 and audio players such as the iPod; digital cameras; and video cameras (Kaiser Family Foundation, 2006).

The role of media literacy in the classroom should not negate the prominent importance of popular culture in the lives of individuals, but instead channel that energy so that it can help to uncover codes and conventions that can be influential, disempowering, and manipulative.

Critical media literacy promises hope for understanding and empowerment. As long as the doorway is open for all viewpoints to come to the table, we can move along the spectrum from cynicism to skepticism and from passivity to power. In order for media literacy to be considered critical literacy, all voices must be heard. There must be a participatory nature to the language of thought. Learning must provide for all voices and perspectives to be heard. These two things are exactly what is suggested for today's classroom instruction. Furthermore, there must be connections to the students' prior knowledge, cultural background, and community in order for critical media literacy to work well in and out of the classroom. Ultimately, the role of the educator many times will be to help students clarify and interpret the media. Without question, the media require a lot of explanation.

REFERENCES

AAP Committee on Communications. 1995. "Children, Adolescents, and Advertising." *Pediatrics,* Vol. 95, No. 2 (February): 295–297.

Center for Media Literacy. 2002. "Five Core Concepts." CML MediaLit Kit. Los Angeles, CA: Center for Media Literacy.

Center for Media Literacy. 2002. "Five Key Questions." CML MediaLit Kit. Los Angeles, CA: Center for Media Literacy.

Kaiser Family Foundation. 2005. "Generation M Media in the Lives of 8–18 Year-Old" (March).

Kaiser Family Foundation. 2006. "The Teen Media Juggling Act: The Implications of Media Multitasking Among American Youth" (December).

Nielsen Survey. 2005. "Average American Family TV Viewing" (September).

Potter, James. 2005. *Media Literacy.* Thousand Oaks, CA: Sage Publications.

Rubin, Richard. 2004. *Foundations of Library Science and Information Science,* 2nd ed. New York: Neal-Schuman.

Share, Jeff. 2002. "What Media Literacy Is Not." CML MediaLit Kit, 21. Los Angeles, CA: Center for Media Literacy.

Silverblatt, Art. 2001. *Media Literacy: Keys to Interpreting Media Messages.* Westport, CT: Praeger Publishers.

2 UNDERSTANDING THE SIGNIFICANCE OF MEDIA LITERACY FOR STUDENTS

> "Increasingly, our students' experience of the world is one mediated by the communication cornucopia that makes up their electronic environment."
>
> —*David Considine*

STUDENTS' CONSUMPTION OF MEDIA

There is no question that media is a part of students' daily lives. The Kaiser Family Foundation and The Family and Community Critical Viewing Project have compiled statistics that, while shocking, also indicate the integral role the media have played in children's lives. Here are just a few statistics to consider:

- Forty-seven percent of children ages six through seventeen have a TV in their own bedrooms. This figure has not changed, but it now includes younger children. Just a decade ago, TV would not even be considered in a small child's bedroom. That has changed. Currently, 23 percent of children from ages one to five are fully equipped with television and a VCR or DVD player (Kaiser Family Foundation, 2005).

- By the age of eighteen, children have watched 17,000 hours of television, and this number continues to increase. Oddly enough, this figure has not decreased even with the introduction of computers and Instant Messaging. What has changed is that the age group of viewers now includes younger children, while middle schoolers multitask—using the Internet while watching or listening to their favorite media (American Academy of Pediatrics, 2001).

Much like the discussion in the Calvin and Hobbes comic strip in Figure 2-1, the latest Nielsen research indicates that the average home has the television on for seven and half hours per day. This means the television is on nearly sixty hours per week. This figure is astronomical considering the time students are in school and the amount of time that

Figure 2-1. "TV Viewing" by Bill Watterson
(**CALVIN AND HOBBES** © 1997 Watterson. Dist. By Universal Press Syndicate.
Reprinted with permission. All rights reserved.)

they sleep. Even the amount of time children sleep has declined since television was introduced into the bedroom. How is seven hours of TV viewing a day even possible? Consider that throughout the study, many families reported that the TV is turned on as soon as they are awake and then as soon as the first person enters the home in the afternoon. In many cases, the first person home is the child. Afternoon programming is targeted directly at the youngest members of the family. After 3 PM, most shows are comedies, cartoons, or light dramas. The commercials that run from 3 PM to 6 PM are specifically targeted to this group. Most commercials for toys, junk food, and "kid friendly" restaurants such as McDonald's appear during this time period. After 6 PM, the commercials and the programming begin to switch to a more adult audience. This is also the average family's dinner hour. Seventy percent of families today eat dinner with the TV on, thus lessening direct conversation and interaction.

With news programs dominating the 6 PM time slot, car and prescription drug commercials fill the airwaves. It is important to note that car commercials are no longer directed solely to parents but also have the children in mind. Many car companies have realized that they have a greater market if they can convince the children to influence their parents' buying trends. Many new gadgets have been adapted and included in order to suggest that their highest commodity, the child, will be most comfortable or most entertained. It certainly speaks to the statistic that finds that children ages four through twelve spent nearly $20 billion "of their own money" during any given year and are influencing their families to spend billions more (Schor 2004, 21).

THE INFLUENCE OF MEDIA

The American Academy of Pediatrics has done a number of studies that detail violence in the media. They found that the average child sees 13,000 violent deaths on TV during his or her formative years and as many as 200,000 by their eighteenth birthday. It is not surprising, then, to learn that the greater number of accidents with children also happen during those years. More important, since children view these programs and their experiences are not discussed in detail within their families, they tend to copy what they see in their play and with their friends. In some ways, this is beneficial in terms of dealing with the content, but it also means that by duplicating what they are seeing they are also involved in some very destructive behavior, as evidenced by the following incidents:

- In 2002, a boy in Seattle, Washington, set himself on fire after attempting to emulate a stunt done on the program *Jackass*, which was produced on MTV. While the program carries many warnings that the tricks should not be duplicated, consider the audience of viewers. This child suffered third-degree burns (Reuters, 2002).
- In a similar incident a year prior, a thirteen-year-old boy in Connecticut allowed two friends to pour gasoline on his legs and feet and set him on fire after seeing a similar stunt on television. He suffered second- and third-degree burns (Associated Press, 2001).
- In May 1999, a seven-year-old boy in Dallas, Texas, killed his three-year-old brother after imitating a pro wrestling move he saw on television. Wrestling moves have been the cause of several violent deaths of young children as well as early teens (Associated Press, 1999).

This idea of "suspended belief" is what doctors call when children view violent events and do not realize the consequences of the actions portrayed in fiction versus reality. This is a very real phenomenon that exemplifies the need for media literacy training in all ages.

The items listed above are, of course, the examples of some of the worst in media, but there are also the opposite. Children of all ages will proclaim that the media that they listen to, watch, or partake in are just fun entertainment and that they would not want them disturbed. David Considine, a professor at Appalachian State University who coined the phrase "putting the 'me' in media," exemplifies this attitude (Considine 2002, 6). This phrase basically means that the media are about the individual children or students and their media likes and dislikes, not about whether we as educators like what they are immersing themselves in within this context.

Students have a wide variety of choice when it comes to media preferences. They can select different genres of music or different artists, or they can mix and match many genres and artists. Television offers the same wide variety of selections, even if the choices are not always what adults consider to be the best. Clothing, jewelry, and other elements of pop culture become a unique part of choice. Students can easily place themselves in the media sphere, and they do so quite readily. Because it is such an important part of their landscape, the importance of being able to deconstruct what they see, hear, buy, or select makes the teaching of media literacy valuable. In the classroom, the topic of media provides the opportunity for healthy conversation to take place, where students can agree and disagree over content and material and where an educator can interject and offer another avenue of thinking.

THE T.A.P. MODEL

One of the best ways to pull students into the conversation and to open doors is through the use of the T.A.P. Model: Text, Audience, and Production. The model was developed by Eddie Dick, Media Education Officer for the Scottish Film Council (Duncan, 1996).

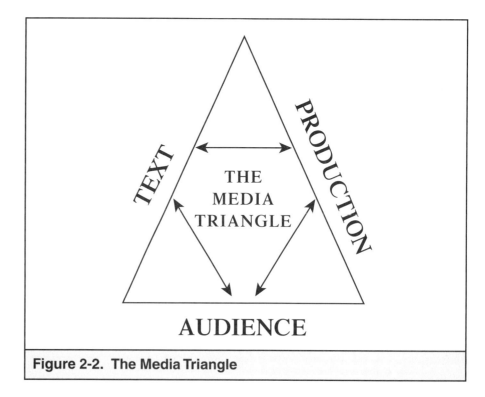

Figure 2-2. The Media Triangle

The model stresses analysis and practice within a cultural, political, and economic milieu. The audience component of the model acknowledges the current research emphasis on audience response theory and the active use of media by the audience. The production component examines who produces media, and how it is distributed, as well as the technical, economic and legal issues at work in producing media products. The text component reveals intended meaning and other, more hidden, meanings as well as genre, values, narrative and issues which cue the meaning of media content (The Strategies for Media Literacy Inc Quarterly, 1989).

Text:

- In what ways does this text tell a story? Does it connect to a larger story?
- What codes and conventions are used?
- What are the characters like? Are they realistic? Are they stereotypes?
- Is there an expected running time for a film or song? Are there any copyright or trademarks used to protect certain words or products?
- How do the characters relate to each other in terms of power, age, gender, race, and class?
- What are the values and ideology of the characters? To what extent do I share these beliefs?

Audience:

- How does this text appeal to me? What things do I like and dislike?
- Who is the intended target audience?
- How and why does this text appeal to its audience?
- In what different ways do people use or consume this text?
- How could I change the text to make it more enjoyable?

Production:

- Where does this text come from? Who created it? Who owns it?
- How is this text distributed or sold to the public? Who profits?

- How was the text made? What production techniques were used?
- What rules and laws affect this text?
- Is there an expected running time for a film or song? Are there any copyrights or trademarks used to protect certain words or products?
- How could I produce a similar text? (Duncan, 1996).

THE PLEASURE PRINCIPLE

Another benefit of teaching media literacy is how readily students want to contribute to the conversation. It is amazing how many opinions they have on a wide variety of topics because it is a meaningful part of their environment. It certainly surprised me when a student and I argued over the merits of his choice of musical artist. The artist in question was Eminem. The student professed that Eminem was not beholden to the marketing gimmicks epitomized by other artists in the same music genre. When we broke down how music reached the mainstream and what artists had to do in order for their music to be heard it became obvious quickly that the student's supposition could not be true. However, much of the student's argument was based upon this musician's lyrics, which he found to be profound. He had some very clear points for why he considered this artist to be unlike any of the more generic ones in society. More important, I had realized that my approach was all wrong because I had not understood this idea of the "pleasure principle." When I was able to step back and accept this student's beliefs, then we could have a crucial and thoughtful discussion.

The "pleasure principle" is as basic as it sounds. Each of us likes and dislikes many different elements of media. For our students, the same is true even if we don't necessarily "get it." The point becomes less about getting it as it is about understanding why it makes more sense to them and less to us. Also, it provides an opportunity for other ideas to be introduced and discussed. One of the highlights of my teaching career was when a high school student returned to me two years after taking a media literacy course with me in middle school and told me she understood the word "propaganda" because of my class. The exchange of ideas is an important part of the process. Literacy training only comes with conversation, and teens, most especially, need a platform for the plethora of ideas that mainstream media have generated.

Understandably, popular culture texts may not always be easy to deal with or even be ones that we as educators are comfortable discussing. The importance of stepping out of our comfort zone, however, cannot be emphasized enough. Our students are in need of educators who can venture into their "play" areas in order to grasp what they are experiencing. We cannot ignore how our teen/young adult audience negotiates meaning.

THE IMPORTANCE OF CRITICAL THINKING

For young adults, the need to learn how to deal with media messages has never been more prevalent. The amount of media consumed by this generation of students necessitates their learning how the media construct our understanding of issues, products, people, gender, and race. The images and messages presented from television, pictures, or advertisements are constant and continuous. These media texts are significant to the daily lives of teens, and education about those messages needs to be more consistent in schools.

This approach in critical thinking allows students to incorporate their own understanding and interpretation of what they have seen, heard, read, and watched while at the same time taking into account why it is that they find pleasure in that particular form of media. One of the goals of media literacy is to teach students to be critical thinkers about all media textual formats. Critical viewing is important and has an applicable and valid place in today's classroom environments. Children are regularly exposed to media in which the intention is to manipulate their opinions. Thus, learning to evaluate their own responses to what they are experiencing is very important. With instructional guidance, they can be encouraged to explore the reasons for their reactions and the techniques being used.

Art Silverblatt, from the Department of Communication and Journalism at Webster University, suggests that "analysis hinges on a reference point of personal experience, through which individuals can examine the impact of the media on their attitudes, values, lifestyles and personal decisions" (Silverblatt, 2001). The prior knowledge of each individual child on any given topic will determine the amount of critical analysis needed. A child's religious, economic, or political upbringing impacts how a text or message is viewed and interpreted. Students come into the classroom with various backgrounds which influence their reading and comprehension. The range of knowledge is smaller in the elementary grades, but as children move toward high school this changes tremendously because of the exposure students have to a variety of different texts. This does not necessarily mean that what they know is accurate or that each student has had the same amount of background knowledge, but it does mean that their experiences are greater. While this reference appears to apply only to print resources, the same principles apply to other media. For example, a middle or high school child watching a program such as *Will and Grace* would be faced with many issues such as sexuality that would conflict with certain religious beliefs or even economic ones, while other children would not find conflict in these behaviors. Another popular television show, *Lizzie McGuire,* which fascinates many white, middle-class children, is not popular with other racial groups. Family issues are another questionable topic because the stereotypes shown on television and in other media certainly do not reflect reality. Some of the texts could be interpreted based upon cultural beliefs and could be offensive to one student while having no effect on another. Many popular songs and their artists are emulated by children and can also cause controversy. One example is Britney Spears, who was marketed as a teenage "virgin" and then switched gears, horrifying many parents.

The high volumes of mediated messages students consume, whether accurate or not, add tremendously to their background knowledge of the world. From television to radio, magazines, newspapers, billboards, and movies, the bombardment of information is extremely high, yet very few people challenge the messages that students receive. The importance of children's ability to be critical thinkers has never been more important than now.

REFERENCES

AAP Committee on Communications. 1995. "Media Violence." *Pediatrics,* Vol. 95, No. 6 (June): 949–951.

AAP Committee on Communications. 2001. "Children, Adolescents, and Television," *Pediatrics*, Vol. 107, No. 2 (February): 423–425.

Associated Press. 2001. "Teen Burned Imitating MTV Stunt" (January 29). Available at: www.associatedpress.com

Considine, David. 2002. "Putting the ME in MEdia Literacy." *Middle Ground: The Magazine of Middle Level Education,* 6 (October): 15–21.

Considine, David, and Gail Hailey. 1992. *Visual Messages Integrating Imagery into Instruction.* Englewood, CO: Libraries Unlimited.

Duncan, Barry. 1996. *Mass Media and Popular Culture.* Toronto: Harcourt-Brace Publishers.

Kaiser Family Foundation. 2005. "Generation M Media in the Lives of 8–18 Year-Old" (March).

Reuters. 2002. "Teen Burns Himself Copying 'Jackass' Stunt" (November 1). Available at: www.reuters.com

Schor, Juliet. 2004. *Born to Buy: The Commercialized Child and the New Consumer Culture.* New York: Scribner.

Silverblatt, Art. 2001. *Media Literacy: Keys to Interpreting Media Messages.* Westport, CT: Praeger Publishers.

Tristani, Gloria. 1999. "Wrestling for Our Children's Future." Remarks of the FCC Commissioner before the Congress on Television Violence (October 12). Available at: www.fcc.gov/Speeches/Tristani/spgt916.doc

3 ADDING MEDIA LITERACY INTO THE CURRICULUM

> "Meeting the demands of the 21st century requires more than content knowledge. In order to provide both flexibility and security in an era characterized by constant change, 21st century students need "knowing how to learn" skills that enable them to acquire knowledge and skills, connect new information to existing knowledge, analyze, develop habits of learning and work with others to use the information."
> —*Partnership for 21st Century Skills, 2002*

Information literacy and media literacy curriculums have been in constant motion since the 1970s. The need for students to handle a variety of data sources and to critically think about the information that they obtain, either through their own personal use of media or from what they obtain from libraries or the Internet, has never been more important. Certainly the role of the school library media specialist has had to change to accommodate the ways in which people are processing, evaluating, and producing information. Questions regarding accuracy, clarity, and responsible use are becoming widely prevalent, which begets the development of curriculums that can cover the scope of these questions. A media literacy curriculum provides the school library media specialist and classroom teacher with a way to cover a whole area of media vehicles and the messages that they produce as information.

Already, the twenty-first century has brought about many technological changes that have shaped the media habits of our students. This technology has altered and changed the ways in which we teach our students. In fact, if we were to look at what the classroom of the early 1990s was and compare it to today, there are some significant changes, from how we communicate with our peers to how we provide lessons for our students. In order to understand where media literacy fits into the curriculum, it is important to have a historical perspective on what has been instituted in our school and home environments that has changed this generation of learners.

As computers were introduced into our culture in the 1980s, other technological items such as the Walkman and videogames developed by Atari and Coleco also became standard. In the 1990s, desktop computers became laptops and video games became more aggressive, detailed, and even violent with newer game systems such as Sony's Playstation, Microsoft's X-Box, and Nintendo's Game Cube. At the turn of the twenty-first century, many of these systems became faster and more complex. Instead of using floppy disks to transport data from our computers, we had burnable discs and now flash drives which are smaller than a tube of lipstick. The Walkman has all but left us. Children of all ages listen to iPods and MP3 players, with their crisp and clear sound.

THE MEDIA LITERACY GAP

With all of these new advances in the realm of technology, it would seem rather obvious to think that schools have incorporated some, if not all, of these technologies into their curriculums. Unfortunately, schools have fallen slowly and steadily behind and many of the curriculums that we see across the United States lag in terms of understanding and using these technologies. The only steadfast pieces that have continued to be in use are TVs and VCRs or DVDs, although the media literacy component of what could possibly be taught is usually lost. In many classrooms, teachers show entire films with very little discussion. The opportunities for analysis and evaluation can be easily neglected. While our students have gained access to many different programs, schools are hampered by financial woes or gaps in the teaching community which have not been overcome.

In the global community, the United States is also looked upon as being latent and even regressive in the integration of media literacy into the classroom curriculum. While in countries such as Canada, England, and Australia media literacy has become a defined area of study, in this country the work has just begun. Marshall McLuhan, a Canadian academic who during the 1960s wrote *Understanding Media*, became a founding father in the study of media literacy when he commented, "The medium is the message" (McLuhan 1964, 23). McLuhan predicted that technology and media would grow at a rapid pace and that schools needed to adapt techniques for students to learn and process the information they were receiving by what at that time were only television and radio. As a university professor, he could easily see that his students were consumed by the media but that he had not kept up. In many ways, this observation changed his life and his belief that the media were to change all our lives.

In some communities of learning, media literacy is sometimes looked at as a separate subject area, but it is a tool best used in combination with the school curriculum. As Elizabeth Thoman, the founder of the Center for Media Literacy, states, "Media Literacy is not a new subject to teach, but a new way to teach all subjects" (Center for Media Literacy, 2002–2003). The media permeate all content areas. It is very hard to believe that schools have been able to keep from teaching about the media and popular culture, especially when you consider that the media have long been dominating the educational infrastructure, but that is exactly what has happened.

The topics shaped by the media seem to breed fear in teachers because they are afraid to deal with the questions that may arise from the discussion. There is also a worry that they would not know what their students are talking about on any given topic. This fear more than any other has caused for much of this type of instruction to not take place in the classroom. In part this is because the role of the teacher has long been as the leader of the classroom. Media literacy provides for a wide spectrum of ideas to be exchanged, in which a student is sometimes the leader or guide and the teacher takes a step back and allows the student to take a step forward.

While this concept may seem natural for some teachers, for others this is most difficult. In media literacy, the teacher becomes more of a guide, one who may pose the question that needs to be discussed but also the one who will redirect the conversation in order to open different avenues of thinking. This way of teaching is not always comfortable, nor is it easy. However, the best way to know that the material covered in the classroom is reaching students is to see how motivated they are to be in charge of their learning, especially on topics that are of most interest to them. A colleague of mine related to me recently how he taught a lesson on musical artists in the science classroom. His lesson was on truth versus fiction of scientific data as suggested by movies and television shows. The students approached him at the end of the school year and told him that they were thrilled to have a modern-day topic used for discussion, and they thought it was "cool" that he had broached the subject using popular culture texts.

THE PARTNERSHIP FOR 21st CENTURY SKILLS

Today's schools are in need of adapting twenty-first-century skills. Twenty-first-century skills deal specifically with higher-order thinking as applied to new technologies, therefore changing the way students are taught in schools nationwide. There are many guides developed by media specialists and teachers to facilitate this learning. One of these guides is the Partnership for 21st Century Skills.

The Partnership for 21st Century Skills is both a guide and a group of individuals from the private and public sectors, which includes a diverse group of teachers and business professionals from all over the country. They gathered together to address their concerns on what they believed a twenty-first-century student should look like and what schools should be doing in order to accomplish the goal of educating that student. In their first report, presented in 2000, they indicated that we have a growing community of learners that use technology on a regular basis, but our schools, while attempting to, are unable, or in some cases unwilling, to reinforce the skills learned. We know that students understand podcasting, know how to blog, Instant Message (IM) each other on a regular basis, play intricate and detailed video games, and so much more. Yet, if we were to ask a classroom teacher, and even a library media specialist, to demonstrate the same knowledge, many of them cannot. Instead, our focus has been on the regular classroom instruction, which has not kept up with the new waves of technology in use. Due to the slow change in education, a gap has been created. In five years, it has only closed slightly, in part because of the reluctance of educators to include discussions and lessons on media and technology that would shift the way our students are taught.

Donna Alvermann, Jennifer Moon, and Margaret Hagwood, in their book *Popular Culture in the Classroom,* state, "texts and literate practices of everyday life are changing at an unprecedented and disorienting pace" (Alvermann, Moon, and Hagwood, 1999:4). Media literacy is a skill that can help students decipher the massive amount of information sent through the various media. There is no question that the world is moving at a very fast pace, and the classroom of tomorrow must be ready to do the same. This conclusion is agreed upon by the Partnership for 21st Century Skills, whose charge was to find curricular connections that would bring students closer to a place where they can work and live in a community where the media, technology, and other multimedia platforms are a part of their daily lives. As the Partnership for 21st Century Skills commented in their report, the question paramount to educators everywhere is, How can public education better prepare students for the twenty-first century? Their definition of twenty-first-century skills was "teaching through the use of relevant real-world examples, applications and settings to frame academic content for students, enabling them to see the connection between their studies and the world in which they live" (Partnership for 21st Century Skills, 2002). This is exactly what media literacy does in the classroom and why it is considered a twenty-first-century learning skill.

Their initial work provided resources that demonstrated the bridge of learning for improving learning and education. They made claim to six elements of twenty-first-century learning:

- Emphasize core subjects.
- Emphasize learning skills.
- Use twenty-first-century tools to develop learning skills.
- Teach and learn in a twenty-first-century context.
- Teach and learn in a twenty-first-century content.
- Use twenty-first-century assessments that measure core subjects and twenty-first-century skills (Partnership for 21st Century Skills, 2002).

The Partnership for 21st Century Skills provided a comprehensive framework which developed cocurricular ideas in all the core subject areas, which they hoped would benefit students and teachers alike in the classroom. An email address will be given at the end of the book to help you follow up on some of the work that they have done, and it also links to an information and communications technologies (ICT) framework of how these skills fit into the content areas.

CURRICULUM CONNECTIONS

Media literacy should be fully incorporated into the classroom and used in a variety of ways with the curricular topics as questions regarding media arise throughout the academic school year. The best part of teaching about the media is that the media provide many of the lessons that would fit into any curriculum, any given week. Media literacy topics can range from January's Superbowl to November's election season. A discussion about the release of a new *Harry Potter* book, the Olympics, the war in Iraq, journalists who write fictional stories, the recall of a prescription drug, or the cost of ads and the types of ads can happen in almost any area of study. These topics are real and have initiated wide discussions in my own classrooms.

We do want our children to be critical viewers and critical consumers of the media, but unlike what students may believe, most school library media specialists and classroom teachers are not trying to ruin the entertainment value of students' media. It is important that we acknowledge that the media bring enjoyment to the student audience. Therefore, to discuss their medium means to respect that there is a need to respect their choices even if, as educators, we don't like those choices or consider some programs or media a negative in their lives.

The point is that media literacy in the curriculum is about sharing an experience while teaching and learning how it affects the recipient of the message. When dealing with a controversial musical artist or a controversial television program such as *South Park*, how do you begin a conversation that is respectful yet at the same time meaningful to all present? It requires that our preconceived opinions take a step back so that we can listen to what students think. A way to start is by asking students to give their general opinion and then have a student take the lead on how the music or the program affects different audiences. The important aspect of this discussion is to remember that the media we are discussing are a very personal part of each of our students' lives.

What educators need to avoid is demoralizing or bashing a favored media artist or medium because of a difference in taste. David Considine, a professor at Appalachian State University, discusses this in terms of the "pleasure principle." Students will rebel if they believe that choices are attacked, and instead will not participate in any discussion then or in the future and will shut out the instructor. It is something that he experienced himself when at a presentation to teens (Considine, 2002). Teachers can have meaningful positive and critical conversations on many aspects of media as long as they show consideration to the intended audience.

Most schools today are feeling the enormous weight of carrying extra subjects while also maintaining a core program. The idea of another literacy being introduced into the curriculum causes many teachers to feel apprehensive and certainly does not motivate them to include it in their curriculum. This is exactly where the media specialist enters, in order to provide knowledge and understanding on how to incorporate all literacies in the various subject areas.

The role of the school library media specialist is crucial in determining how curriculum gets delivered to the student body through the classroom teacher. Also, providing this service to the community of teachers allows for some of the weight of instruction to be taken off and shared in collaboration with the classroom teaching. Collaboration is one of the most important traits of a school library media specialist, and this topic will be covered further in the following chapter.

In order for the curriculum to move forward, the main objective is to have an administrative and teaching staff which realizes that popular culture has a place in the current curriculum. They must also understand the powerful influence these lessons can have in changing the classroom dynamic. There are many lessons to be learned from how students are adapting and interacting with the media.

How can a media specialist and classroom teacher work collaboratively to incorporate media literacy lessons? The following chapter will give specific lesson examples designed to incorporate teaching media literacy in the content areas.

REFERENCES

Alvermann, Donna, Jennifer Moon, and Margaret Hagwood. 1999. *Popular Culture in the Classroom: Teaching Researching Critical Media Literacy*. New York: International Reading Association.

Center for Media Literacy. 2002–2003. "Getting Started: Strategies for Introducing Media Literacy in Your School or District." Available at: www.medialit.org/pd_getting_started.html (accessed August 11, 2006).

Considine, David. 2002. "Putting the ME in MEdia Literacy." *Middle Ground: The Magazine of Middle Level Education*, No. 6 (October): 15–21.

McLuhan, Marshall. 1964. *Understanding Media: The Extensions of Man*. New York: McGraw-Hill, 1964.

Partnership for 21st Century Skills. 2002. "Learning for the 21st Century: A Report and Mile Guide for 21st Century Skills."

Partnership for 21st Century Skills. 2004. Available at: www.21stcentury skills.org (accessed September 23, 2006).

PROVIDING MEDIA LITERACY IN THE SCHOOL LIBRARY AND CONTENT AREA CLASSROOMS

> "If we strive to teach students the best way to critically evaluate the information that they find in relation to the purpose at hand, we will produce a generation of digitally literate adults who are equipped to learn throughout their lifetimes. In the end, is this not the greatest lesson we can teach today's students?"
>
> —*Kathleen Schrock*

Where does the school library media program fit in your school? Is it the center, the collaborator, the hub of knowledge, the place where all the media are kept? Whether the library is one or all of these to your school environment, media literacy instruction fits well into your school's curriculum. The role of the media specialist is crucial in promoting media literacy lessons. As the keeper of the school's media, the school librarian has the opportunity to share knowledge as well as demonstrate an understanding of media's impact on today's youth.

In a world in which information is transmitted at a rapid speed and images fly across television screens in seconds, it is important to have lessons to help students distinguish information in order to process what is "mainstream." Media literacy affords the media specialist an opportunity to bring into the classroom a variety of texts which fit into the content areas while teaching literacy skills that help teach our students to analyze, evaluate, and deconstruct in collaboration with the classroom teacher.

The American Association of School Librarians (AASL) has been seeking to promote these skills through their definition of information literacy: "A transformational process in which the learner needs to find, understand, evaluate, and use information in various forms to create for personal, social, or global purposes." (AASL, 1999) AASL broadens the definition through the concept of critical thinking by stating, "students need to be better observers, appliers, and evaluators of ideas and information. . . . The ability to think critically appears to be cross-disciplinary, training approaches for students can and should be incorporated into many curricular areas" (AASL, 1999). Media literacy asks students to question the common perceptions and push the analysis further.

Media literacy is the ability to understand how the different forms of mass media work, how they produce meanings, how they are organized, and how to use them wisely. The media-literate person is proficient in describing the role media play in his or her life, can distinguish the basic conventions of various media, and enjoys his or her use consciously. This defines what teachers and library media specialists can teach together through content and through teachable moments presented by the media and students daily.

School library media specialists are always looking for ways to get their community of teachers to explore new territories and new forms of teaching. Media literacy instruction offers such an opportunity. The teacher and the school library media specialist can share the task while having a classroom of alert and interested students.

One of the best advantages of taking on teaching media literacy techniques and questioning is that it lends itself to what children are most interested in: television, film, the Internet, music, and video games. For example, if a classroom of students are told that the teacher is going to talk about advertisements in science class (and yes, let's talk about all those drug ads out there), most of the hands in the classroom will be up and shaking. Students can also recite the slogans and jingles to most advertisements. Ask students, What does all of that language mean, and Can you list all the advertisements you have seen? During a social studies unit on the 1920s, early film can be used. The classroom teacher can discuss the political and social dynamics of the time while the media specialist reviews the social and technological period. (As a side note, the 1920s are a period of history which offers great media history opportunities. The development of film and sound in this decade pushed the media world forward.)

How do you convince classroom teachers that they need to work on promoting other literacy skills? Ask them. Believe it or not, it wasn't difficult to do in my school. Most teachers are aware of the fact that students are more interested in the media they use than in the curriculum set for them by schools. Suggesting ways to incorporate both can almost guarantee better student participation and interest in the topics. In addition, many classroom teachers are overloaded, and they are always willing to share the responsibility of teaching as long as they don't have to deviate from their curriculums.

There were a few skeptics in my building, but after we started one successful project, more teachers signed on. The benefit for the library media specialist working collaboratively with a classroom teacher is twofold: besides promoting a valuable program, having two teachers keeps disciplinary problems at bay and allows more time for meaningful work with students. The classroom teacher will appreciate that aspect as much as all the rest. AASL has promoted this concept of collaboration in standards which state:

> School library media specialists model and promote collaborative planning with classroom teachers in order to teach concepts and skills of information processes integrated with classroom content. They partner with other education professionals to develop and deliver an integrated information skills curriculum. (AASL, 1999)

Below are a few other ideas for using media literacy within five major content areas: social studies, science, language arts, math, and foreign language. Each of the lessons described have been used in my own middle school classrooms, and all of them were taught in collaboration with the classroom teacher.

SOCIAL STUDIES

Most students are familiar with some of the big blockbuster historical epics such as *The Patriot* and *Pearl Harbor*. However, the history behind the story gets convoluted because of the emphasis on the secondary storyline. Although many filmmakers try very hard to stay true to the historical time-line, we know they miss at times. There are several occasions when this can be tested. For example, when covering the Civil War there are great programs demonstrating the burning of Atlanta. Ken Burns produced a television series called *The Civil War* which had detailed sketched drawings of what occurred during this time period. Those drawings could be compared with the same account shown in the movie *Gone with the Wind*. Analyze which was more accurate by asking questions such as:

- How are the images different?
- What makes the message powerful in each case?
- What captivates an audience in each case?
- How did the producers or directors of each piece work at bringing about accurate detail to this historical event?

Another place to get historical data is through programs offered by A&E such as the *History Channel* or the *Discovery Channel*. A&E produced a program entitled *The Civil War Journal* which devotes a lengthy portion to Alexander Gardner and the war photographer's use of the new medium of camera photography. Gardner's photographs captured some of the most disturbing images of the Civil War. Photography is an incredible tool to use in classrooms. Students enjoy the production component. Images are captivating to students of all ages. The Civil War offers openings to teach many topics such as how photography has developed, photo manipulation, and censorship, while also considering a comparative analysis of war photos seen today.

One of the best places to keep up with programs on cable or even movie events such as the ones just described is a resource entitled *Cable in the Classroom (CIC)*. *CIC* is a monthly magazine with ideas of how to use educational programming in the classroom. The magazine also provides a schedule of when programs will air, copyright information, and the length of time that a program can be held by a school library or a classroom. Each month a teacher, a school librarian, or other educators are highlighted along with programs they have incorporated into their content areas.

SCIENCE

The media encourage consumers to make inaccurate assumptions about products that can easily be investigated through the science classroom. Advertisements seek to convince the public that the product will make our life better. Advertisements for products such as shampoos and detergents make generalized claims that the products are "new and improved" or "soft and gentle" on your skin. How about products delivered to the public as being "pH balanced" or "no harsh ingredients"? Using chemistry, the science teacher and the media specialist can teach students to evaluate the advertisement's claims through instruction on chemical classifications and product testing: the perfect lesson!

Health and food consumption are big topics in schools. Lessons can demonstrate how food artistry impacts how visually attracted people can be to advertisements. Students can look at ingredients on packages of foods that are advertised as "all natural" or "heart healthy" and compare that with what they know about normal, healthy, and balanced eating habits.

Another important discussion to have in the classroom involves the prescription drug advertisements. Many students know the names of these products and can tell you what the advertisers state they can remedy, but they don't understand the idea of fine print and certainly not how this mass marketing of drugs has changed the whole health industry.

LANGUAGE ARTS

Several books may be considered for classroom read-alouds. Linda Ellerbee's series *Girl Reporter* is best for upper elementary grades, *The Gospel According to Larry* and *Vote for Larry* by Janet Tashjian fit the middle school classroom, and *Feed* by M. T. Anderson falls in line with Orwell's *1984* for the high school reader. Each book contains topics related to media consumption, politics, and much more. The lessons that can be taught from these books are plentiful. These books provide collaborative opportunities between the language arts teacher and the media specialist in which each can take the issues presented and develop them to fit the two curriculums. Having two teachers, one covering language arts topics such as theme and point of view and the other looking at the media literacy concepts, makes for a very interactive classroom. Students have written some provocative essays on the topic of media based upon their reflection on these books.

For the younger grades, books such as *Arthur's TV Trouble* by Marc

Brown or *The Berenstain Bears and Too Much TV* by Stan and Jan Berenstain can lead into telling conversations about what children are watching, the amount of television viewed regularly, and even topics of confusion that have come up while watching certain programs.

In the area of writing, one of the best lessons we employed as a collaborative team was a visual literacy program. The program combined images of one of our cities with students taking digital photographs, then analyzing what they learned and incorporating their work into a multimedia presentation. This lesson was much more a production component of media literacy, but it is one that is necessary in teaching how images and ideas are constructed.

MATH

This is another excellent area for developing media literacy skills. Math teachers are always looking for innovative ways of tying their subject area into real life. Most media centers in the United States have newspapers delivered daily as part of the Newspapers in Education program. The *New York Times* also provides an educational program that uses their newspaper in lessons on critical thinking, healthy self-esteem, and drug prevention.

Begin teaching media literacy lessons with something as simple as looking at pricing. What does it cost for advertising and marketing a product before the product is purchased? This is especially important since children, particularly tweens, are now considered a billion-dollar industry by marketers. This teaches students math lessons such as cost and loss while making them savvy consumers.

Introduce statistics by having students document programs watched, hours of the day, and number of times during the week. This helps them to develop the basic principles of collecting data. Once the data are collected, using their results to draw statistical conclusions makes for fascinating classroom discussions while also keeping in line with curriculum expectations.

FOREIGN LANGUAGE

Most people do not consider foreign language relevant to media literacy skills, but it is. How Americans are perceived outside the United States, research projects that look into how our consumer habits have influenced other countries, and lessons that create empathy for people of foreign descent are all opportunities for looking at global issues.

At the high school level, foreign policy is a key issue to cover with students. Looking at the United Nations and its impact on our world and understanding how an international perspective on the world explains our history and our relations with foreign governments are lessons that provide greater understanding of communities. Stereotyping and bias are two other topics that need to be covered. *In the Mix*, a PBS production that uses high schoolers as reporters, has done an excellent job of engaging teens with topics that relate to the media and to the culture of youth. One of their best programs was developed after September 11th. *The New Normal* was a three-part series that not only looked at the media's coverage of this disastrous event but also covered the teens who worked and lived near Ground Zero and the topic of dealing with differences specific to the Islamic and Sikh cultures. These are just a few important lessons that involve media literacy and globalization.

While there are other subjects taught in schools, these are the five main subjects most frequently found in curriculum write-ups and within the education national standards. Media literacy skills are adaptable to all areas and can be used for many more than those presented here, but this a starting point.

When looking at all the ways to incorporate media literacy, there is no question that it has a definitive place in our school libraries and in our classrooms. Media literacy works best as a collaborative endeavor between classroom teacher and library media specialist. The need for such literacy instruction is apparent and is evident in classrooms based upon what students discuss and bring into the schools. Use those conversations and those moments as teachable moments, and consider making the library media center another avenue for supplementing further learning through the use of media literacy.

The following chapters will provide topical lessons to try as a starting point. Adjust any of these lessons to fit into your curriculum area and within your time constraints.

REFERENCE

American Association of School Librarians (AASL). 1999. "Information-Literacy Resources, Standards, and a Research Toolbox for Students." *SLMR Online*. Available at: www.ala.org/aasl (accessed December 2005).

READY-TO-TEACH LESSONS

TELEVISION

> "Television is teaching all the time. It does more educating than the schools and all the institutions of higher learning."
>
> —*Marshall McLuhan*

> "American children between the ages of six and eleven watch an average of 26 hours of television a week; by the time a child graduates from high school, she or he will have watched 22,000 hours of television compared with only 11,000 hours in the classroom."
>
> —*Nielsen TV Rating Service*

Television is a primary source of information for students and adults alike. As the Nielsen Ratings Service has documented, children ages three to eighteen years spend hours upon hours watching television. This means that they are spending more time learning from this medium than any other experience in their lives, including family time. These statistics come as a surprise to many people, including students who attend media literacy classes. While most statistics may seem boring and unimportant to students, statistics related to children are of particular interest to them. Middle school and high school students like to know what the world is saying about them and debate about it. Without question, statistics make great conversation starters to this unit.

- American children between the ages of six and eleven watch an average of 26 hours of television a week; by the time a child graduates from high school, she or he will have watched 22,000 hours of television, compared with only 11,000 hours in the classroom (Nielsen TV Rating Service, 2005).
- The more violence children watch on TV, the more likely they may act in aggressive ways, become less sensitive to others' pain and suffering, and be more fearful of the world around them (PBS Online, 2006)
- The average television program contains five acts of violence per hour; the average children's program shows 25 acts of violence per hour (Turn Off the Violence, 2005).

Many of these statistics will surprise students, and many will deny that this is happening in their home. The point of using these numbers is to generate conversation about television.

The consistent sentiment from many educators is that television is not teaching students anything worthwhile. Television is teaching our children. The real question is, what is it teaching? How do we know if the messages our children are receiving are accurate and informative? This unit bridges many of these concerns by looking at a multitude of television genres. This chapter will look at different programming, the genres, and how to use television in the core content areas.

Grade Level: These lessons have been primarily used in a classroom environment for grades five through eight, but they are adaptable to all grade levels. You determine what best fits your classroom.

This particular grouping of lessons will be broken down by genre: news, sitcoms, drama, talk shows, and reality TV.

Curriculum Connections:	1. English—Reading, writing, and composition
	2. Social Studies—Current events
Media Literacy Connections:	1. Media messages are constructed using a creative language.
	2. Different people experience the same media message differently.
	3. Media have embedded values, lifestyles, points of view, and omissions.
Time Frame:	These lessons can be used in a fifty-minute period. Many of the lessons require students to view a selected television program. You may want to have clips of a predetermined program ready to go in class, in case there are those who do not follow through with the assignment and so you can refer back to the clip during the discussion.

LESSON 5.1: INTRODUCTION TO TELEVISION

Before You Begin

Television today consists of many different types of programs. As there are a variety of genres of books, so too there are a variety of television genres. This initial lesson provides students with an overview of the different forms of programming while also introducing them to television terminology.

Objectives

1. Students will learn how television media messages are constructed.
2. Students will develop a new understanding of television jargon.

Materials

- A ten-minute clip of a compilation of programs. These programs should include sports, news, reality TV, talk shows, cartoons, sitcoms, and dramas.
    - Try to select items that you would expect your students to be watching on a regular basis. If you are not sure what they may be, ask a student.
- You will need copies of the TV terminology sheet found in Supplement 5A.
- You will need copies of the news guide found in Supplement 5B.
- A TV and VCR or DVD player.

Process

- Open class by asking students:
    - What types of television programs do they watch the most?
        - Make a list on the board so that they can see the variety of responses.
- Ask students:
    - What kinds of programs do they currently watch?
        - Make a list on the board so that they can see the variety of responses.
- Show a ten-minute video clip that shows a compilation of programs.
    - Have students make a list of what they are seeing.
- Hand out to students the TV terminology sheet found in Supplement 5A.
- Review all of the terms with students, but primarily the following:

- Affiliate: A small, independently run broadcast house, which is owned by or is attached to a big network. For example, ABC owns hundreds of affiliates all over the country.

- Network: A central point of operations that distributes programming to a number of television stations. For example, NBC headquarters distributes programming to many affiliates.

- Prime time: Peak television viewing time, most often during the evening hours of 8–11 PM on weekdays.

- Newsworthy: Event that is suitably interesting to be reported in a newspaper or the nightly news.

- Teleprompter: A mechanism that scrolls text on a screen, to provide cues for a television anchor or presenter.

• Assign students to watch a television news program using Supplement 5B as their guide.

Assessment

Students will be assessed on classroom participation and interaction with others.

Reflection

This lesson provides the basis for the following lessons on television. It gives students an understanding of the scope of the kinds of programs that air while at the same time giving them a context for the language of television. One of the best aspects of this lesson is that it provides the teachers with some inside knowledge of what their students are viewing on a regular basis. Many times, it is an eye opener for me and it gives me a link to what students consider "cool" programming. This provides insight about why students are saying the things they say and why certain clothing has become the new norm. This is one of the many benefits of teaching media literacy lessons.

LESSON 5.2: WHAT IS NEWS?

Before You Begin

Each of the lessons in this unit requires that students do some television viewing the night prior to the lesson. In this lesson, students should have watched a television news program and used the news guide found in Supplement 5B in order to respond to the class lessons.

Objectives

1. Students will watch news programming and understand the component of a news show.
2. Students will evaluate how news messages are constructed, how news is gathered, and how it is presented.

Materials

- A copy of Supplement 5B for review in class.
- A TV and VCR or DVD player.
- A thirty-minute news broadcast taped and ready to go as part of the discussion.
- A copy of the PBS *In the Mix* program *TV—What You Don't See with Peter Jennings*. This is a four-minute clip that explains how news is selected on a nightly basis for airing.
- You will need copies of the song "News Goo" found in Supplement 5C for classroom discussion.
- You will need copies of the situation comedy guide found in Supplement 5D.

Process

- Begin the lesson by asking students:
  - Why study news?
    - Answer: Students' responses will vary, but mostly they will indicate to stay informed.
  - Do they watch news?
    - Answer: Many students do not watch the news. Some will indicate that they get their news from the Internet.
- Show the video *In The Mix: TV—What You Don't See with Peter Jennings*.
  - The video is approximately four minutes long and gives students a brief insight into how news is developed for broadcast.

- After viewing, ask students for responses on the topics that Peter Jennings covered.
  - Were there any surprises?
    - Answer: Most students will be surprised at the idea that a cameraman can set up a shot so that viewers do not trust the person being filmed.
- Discuss the concept of need to know and right to know.
  - Ask students:
    - What does that mean? How does it affect your perception of the news?
- Have students take out their news guide sheet from the previous evening, Supplement 5B.
- Show students a ten-minute news clip that was recorded from the previous evening.
- Ask students:
  - What were the top news stories?
- Compare the news stories viewed in class with what they viewed in the previous evening.
- Ask students:
  - Was anyone omitted from the news stories? Race? Culture? Whose point of view was missing?
    - Answers will vary.
  - Was there any violence? What kind?
    - Answers will vary.
  - What kinds of commercials aired during their program?
    - Answer: Mostly car and drug commercials air during the news hour because the expectation is that only adults are watching.
- Hand out lyrics of "News Goo" by Polarity 1.
- Break students up in pairs and have them read the lyrics.
- Ask students to answer the following:
  - What is Polarity 1 trying to say in their lyrics?
  - Do they agree or disagree with Polarity 1?
  - Why or why not?
- Briefly introduce the term *situation comedy* (sitcom): normally a thirty-minute comedy in which the characters

remain the same but the situations, mostly based on day-to-day living, change.

- Close class by assigning students to watch a situation comedy (sitcom) that evening, using Supplement 5D as their guide. Include a brainstorm in class so they are sure what a sitcom is on television.

Assessment

Students will be assessed on their completion of the news assignment, Supplement 5B, and their classroom participation.

Reflection

News can be interesting to students when they are asked to see it differently than they did before. The problem is that most often the news is not about them—the teens—and when it is, the news is rarely good. They are definitely one of the audiences omitted from the news and it is worth pointing out what may or may not be an obvious fact to them.

LESSON 5.3: THE SITUATION COMEDY

Before You Begin

Most situation comedies have a family premise and deal with issues that occur in our everyday lives. The difference is that these issues get resolved in under thirty minutes. In our everyday lives, this is almost always impossible. Situation comedies deal with some very serious issues at times, but in a comedic format. Although they clear up matters very quickly, sometimes the information they provide is important. Since their audience is usually young adults, the lessons may have some impact.

Objectives

1. Students will deconstruct how situation comedies reflect day-to-day life situations.
2. Students will analyze the messages conveyed via the situation comedy.

Materials

- A copy of Supplement 5D for review in class.
- A TV and VCR or DVD player.
- A ten- to fifteen-minute clip of a situation comedy to use in class as part of the discussion.
    - Note: Most sitcoms revolve around families, so you should not have too much difficulty in finding one that is appropriate for your class.
- You will need copies of the talk show guide found in Supplement 5E.

Process

- Ask students:
    - What are some of their favorite sitcoms?
        - Put the list on the board so students can see the variety of choices.
- Show the ten- to fifteen-minute clip of your chosen situation comedy.
    - Have students keep notes of the following:
        - Who are the characters? How are the characters connected (family, friends, co-workers)?
        - What is the problem or issue that needs resolution?
    - Note: Make sure that the resolution of the problem is not shown.
- After the clip is completed, ask students:
    - Is the issue realistic?
    - How would they resolve the problem they viewed?
    - Can problems be solved in thirty minutes?
- Break students up into groups of four or five.
- Ask students to share with each other the situation comedies they viewed the night before.
    - Invite students to come up with a general consensus of the problems that arose during their programs.
- Ask one member from each group to share the findings with the class.
- Show how the sitcom you selected resolved its issue.

- Ask students:

  - Is this a reasonable resolution?
  - Would they resolve the same problem in the same way?
  - Is it possible to resolve the issue presented in thirty minutes?

- Close class by assigning students to watch a talk show that afternoon or evening, using Supplement 5E as their guide. Again, brainstorm what fits into the talk show genre.

  - Note: This may be an assignment that requires more than a day's notice as talk show times vary widely. Students may need to set their VCRs or TiVo in advance in order to view their chosen program.

Assessment

Students will be assessed on their completion of the situation comedy assignment, Supplement 5D, and their classroom participation.

Reflection

Students learn a great deal from situation comedies. Because of their amusement factor and because of their many family themes, sitcoms are viewed by the whole family. It is programming that is considered safe and free of any ethical dilemmas. While this may not always be true, the humor is understood by either the child or the adult depending on the situations presented within the program.

LESSON 5.4: THE TALK SHOW

Before You Begin

Talk shows provide entertainment that includes interviews with celebrities as well as everyday people. The success of these programs is evident by how long they have remained on the schedule. Oprah Winfrey has been in the talk show business for over twenty years. Maury Povich, Montel Williams, and many others have also maintained a steady flow of followers. Included in the realm of the talk show are variety shows such as *Regis and Kelly* and *The Jay Leno Show,* which have also created a means of keeping their audience's attention with their celebrity guests and human interest stories. This lesson provides a basis for discussion about why this genre keeps people watching.

Objectives

1. Students will view and evaluate the talk show phenomenon.
2. Students will determine how programming influences the everyday viewing audience.

Materials

- A copy of Supplement 5E for review in class.
- A TV and VCR or DVD player.
- A ten- to fifteen-minute clip of three or four different talk show formats to use in class as part of the discussion.
- Copies of the reality TV guide found in Supplement 5F.

Process

- Open class with a review of topics that they have seen covered on television talk shows.
    - Put a list on the board so that students can see the variety of answers.
        - The list will most likely include some of the following:
            - Divorce
            - Marriage
            - Celebrity Interviews
            - Unusual People
            - Shocking Circumstances
- Show the ten- to fifteen-minute clip of different talk shows.
    - Have students keep track of the topics that came up in each program.
- Ask students:
    - Are these people and situations that you would encounter in your everyday life? Why or why not?

- • Note: Students will agree and disagree in these answers. Make sure that each student listens to the arguments presented.
- Break students up into groups of four or five.
- Ask students to share the talk shows they reviewed with each other.
  - • Ask students to make a list of the guests featured and the problems discussed during their chosen talk show.
- Invite one member from each group to share the findings with the class.
- Close class by assigning students to watch a reality TV show that evening, using Supplement 5F as their guide.

Assessment

Students will be assessed on their completion of the talk show assignment, Supplement 5E, and their classroom participation.

Reflection

Many teachers are often quite surprised by how many students watch talk shows. However, talk shows are programmed to air for the most part in the midafternoon, which is when children are beginning to come home from school. Others are part of the late night schedule and many students will mention watching programming into the early morning hours. This lesson gives the teacher an opportunity to discuss the topics that air while at the same time questioning why someone would appear on a talk show.

LESSON 5.5: REALITY TV

Before You Begin

Reality TV is television's new "pop candy." People are attracted to these programs because the situations are enticing, interesting, or even disgusting. Most middle and high school students will relay to you a number of different reality programs that they are interested in watching. MTV has been a main producer of many programs in this genre. The question is, Do our students believe the messages they are receiving from these programs, and can they delineate between the truth and the editing fiction created by the producers of these programs?

Objectives

1. Students will understand the difference between reality TV and true life realities.
2. Students will deconstruct a reality TV program for classroom analysis.

Materials

- A copy of Supplement 5F for review in class.
- A TV and VCR or DVD player.
- A ten- to fifteen-minute clip of two or three reality TV shows that are most popular with today's teens.
  - Note: Some of the reality TV shows are not appropriate for viewing in a classroom. Be selective when choosing the materials that you use with your students.

Process

- Begin class by asking students:
  - What constitutes a reality TV show?
    - Answer: People are put in everyday or not-so-everyday situations with some rather bizarre people who are made to appear normal, while being watched as to how they behave or interact with others or how they accomplish feats that would not normally occur.
  - How do students know what constitutes such a program?
    - Answers will vary, but most will indicate television advertising or peer review.
  - Why are they popular?
    - Answers will vary, but they will most likely indicate that they are bizarre or unbelievable situations or they like the story line.
- Show the ten- to fifteen-minute clip of the different reality TV shows.
  - Have students keep track of the different programs and the premise for each show.

- Ask students:

  - What makes each of the shows appealing to audiences?

    - Answers will vary.

  - Is this really reality or a fictionalized version of reality?

    - Student response should be very enlightening because there will be a mix of answers. Some students do believe that these situations are real at all times.

  - Do they think they are watching the whole program or selected portions?

    - Answer: Editing is done so that only selected portions are shown; however, students often do not realize this fact.

- Break students up into groups of four or five.
- Ask students to share the reality TV shows they reviewed with each other.

  - Ask students to take notes on the subjects and the situations encountered.

- Invite one member from each group to share the findings with the class.

Assessment

Students will be assessed on their completion of the reality TV assignment, Supplement 5F, and their classroom participation.

Reflection

Reality TV is one of the most popular forms of television for today's youth. They are fascinated with the lives of the people who appear on the shows and the degree of what they are willing to endure. For example, in the television show *Fear Factor* participants will eat or do almost anything to win the contest, and the more disgusting and outrageous the show, the more an audience will tune in to watch. Other programs have followed suit in re-creating a test of limits which seems to be surpassed by each participant. Students will have their own viewpoints as to why this is happening, but more important, it will bring about a discussion of limits and choices.

SUPPLEMENT 5A: TV TERMINOLOGY

Affiliates: Small, independently run broadcast houses all over the country which are owned by or are attached to a big network; for example, ABC owns hundreds of affiliates all over the country.

FCC: The Federal Communications Commission, the organization that regulates what is seen or not seen on television and grants licenses.

Footage: Raw, unedited shots that are taken for television or film.

Network: A central point of operations that distributes programming to a number of television stations; for example, NBC headquarters distributes programming to many affiliates all over the United States.

Newsworthy: Term used to describe an event that is considered suitably interesting to be reported in a newspaper or the nightly news.

Nielsen rating: A measure of what U.S. audiences are watching on television. One point equals one million households.

Prime time: Peak television viewing time, most often during the evening hours of 8–11 PM weekdays.

Public television: Known to most of us as PBS; noncommercial television.

Situation comedy: Also known as a sitcom; normally a thirty-minute comedy in which the characters remain the same but the situations, based on day-to-day living, change.

Syndication: Supplying materials for reuse; in television, this is a way we are able to see programming that has aired from years ago over and over again.

Teleprompter: A mechanism that scrolls text on a screen, to provide cues for a television anchor or presenter.

SUPPLEMENT 5B: NEWS GUIDE

Name:_____

Directions:
Each of you will be watching one of the three big networks for their half-hour news. Select one of the news stations and circle it. It is your choice whether to watch the local or world news. The following is a guide you should use while watching the news.

Note: Read questions before watching the news!

Write down the top three news stories:

1._____

2._____

3._____

From one of the three stories you selected, include who was interviewed for information.

_____

_____

_____

What footage was shown for your selected news story?

_____

_____

_____

Were there any violent images in the top three stories? If yes, explain.

_____

_____

_____

List the commercials shown during the half hour. Whom do you think advertisers are targeting during the news hour?

_____

_____

_____

SUPPLEMENT 5C: "NEWS GOO" BY POLARITY1 LYRICS

Communication Breakdown!
Pause for this message. Wake up!

EVERY STATION IS IDENTIFICATION

Global syndication is shaping the nation. ABC-Disney, NBC-GE.
Murdoch is Foxy and we're the hen, He owns the pen, the camera, the sword.
Buy a Coke, buy a Ford. Getting broke? Getting bored?

What we WANT? What we NEED? What we WANT? What we NEED? Do
we even know who plants the seed? You think the media works for you, But
it's a job for them, they're selling brew. Who owns the media?

Flim-flam diagram, data-jam, handi-cam Caught it, Yo, ya bought it
A mind is a profitable thing to waste. Ya want another taste, baby? WE got

CHORUS: News Goo—What we need to know
News Goo—What we want to know
Get remote control to choose the show. But the more we watch the less we
know
Ignorance grows on the spirit like a tumor . . . till freedom is a rumor

So where's the news of a people left out.
Put a camera in my face just to hear me shout
But they don't wanna hear what I shout about
Ya love it when we're cuffed. But not a people rebuffed
We never play a lead in the sitcom you call the news unless we are accused.

THE POSITIVE REFUSED

It's the poor and unschooled that most need dope but it's the inside dope
that holds the hope
Can't cope with the selling of news like toothpaste. Spitting out headlines
in mad haste.
We gotta stop the flow of news goo keepin' us drunk on a sugary brew in
the Information Age what we lack is information.

JUST A CREW OF HAIRCUTS AND INFO-PRETENSION

With a pun and smile to hold our attention. Like we're a nation of children

Goo Goo is the intention
We are what we eat—we are what we know.

But information is owned by those who own the show
And control the flow. More when we return. Gotta go.

CHORUS: News Goo—What we need to know
News Goo—What we want to know
Get remote control to choose the show. But the more we watch the less we know
Ignorance grows on the spirit like a tumor . . . till freedom is a rumor

Westinghouse and Minnie Mouse in the house.
The future conceived on the bottom line and when the contracts are sorted the truth is aborted.
I'm not a niche group or a fool or a poll.
Their dumbing us down is gonna take its toll.
There's money to be made for making me a pawn.
The bill gets paid when democracy's gone.
With every corporate merge ya know there's a purge.

THEY SPLURGE ON THE DEPT AND THE NEWS GETS THE NET.

The public sector needs a news dissector to separate the hairspray from the Mayday. The Press is supposed to educate, cast light on the snake—not force feed the cake.

But the state of the Press is a crime, it's fake.
500 hundred channels, no reason to rejoice.
We have too much choice and not enough voice.

We now resume our regular programming.

CHORUS: News Goo—What we need to know
News Goo—What we want to know
Get remote control to choose the show. But the more we watch the less we know
Ignorance grows on the spirit like a tumor . . . till freedom is a rumor.

SUPPLEMENT 5D: THE SITUATION COMEDY (SITCOM)

Name:_____

Directions:

You are to watch a sitcom of your choice, as long as it is appropriate for school and use the following guide to comment on what you watched.

Note: Read questions before watching the sitcom!

1. Name of situation comedy selected:_____

2. Network:_____

3. Is your situation comedy syndicated? Circle One. **YES   NO**

4. Give a brief description of the program and the main characters. Tell what night of the week it is on and what age group is most likely to watch this program.

_____

_____

_____

_____

5. What is the family status and economic status in your chosen situation comedy (for example, single, mother or father, children, poor, rich, blended, etc.)?

_____

_____

_____

_____

6. What is the problem taking place with the characters?

_____

_____

_____

7. How was the problem solved? Is this realistic?

_____

_____

_____

SUPPLEMENT 5E: THE TALK SHOW

Talk shows are popular for many reasons. They exist to entertain and to inform. While some have a political or personal motivation, others do not. There are a variety of formats, and some shows are more popular than others.

Note: Read questions before watching the talk show!

Here is a list to choose from:

The Oprah Winfrey Show	*Maury Povich*	*The Daily Show*
The Tonight Show with Jay Leno	*The View*	*Late Night with Conan O'Brien*
The Late Show with David Letterman	*Hannity & Colmes*	*The O'Reilly Factor*
Regis & Kelly	*Montel Williams*	*The Tyra Banks Show*
Good Morning America	*The Today Show*	*The Early Show*
The Dr. Phil Show	*The Rachael Ray Show* Jimmy Kimmel	

1. Name the show you selected and the network.

_____

2. Who is the host of the show? What do you know about him or her?

_____

_____

3. Who were the guests?

_____

_____

_____

4. Why did the guests appear on the show?

_____

_____

_____

_____

_____

5. Was the host or audience, if there is an audience, helpful? How so?

_____

_____

_____

_____

_____

6. What commercials aired during this program?

_____

_____

_____

SUPPLEMENT 5F: REALITY TV

Directions:

Reality TV is the new wave of television programming. Each season, reality TV shows try to dominate the airwaves. Some are successful and some are not. This is an opportunity to evaluate why these programs captivate audiences. You are to select one reality television show to watch. Use the following questions as your guide.

Note: Read questions before watching the show!

There are many shows that have reality-based themes. Here are a few ideas, but you are welcome to choose others. Please confer with me prior to viewing:

Fear Factor	*Big Brother*	*America's Got Talent*
American Idol	*The Amazing Race*	*The Biggest Loser*
Dancing with the Stars	*Survivor*	*The Apprentice*
MTV's Real World	*America's Next Top Model*	*Supernanny*

1. Name the show that you are viewing: _____

2. What network is your program on? _____

3. What nights of the week and times? _____

4. Who is the intended audience for your program?

_____

5. What is the premise of the show?

_____

_____

_____

6. What captured your attention to consider watching this program?

_____

_____

_____

7. Do you consider what you are watching to be "reality?" Why or why not?

_____

_____

_____

8. Would you ever consider participating in a reality TV show? Why or why not?

_____

_____

_____

REFERENCES

BOOKS

AAP Committee on Communications. 2001. "Children, Adolescents, and Television." _Pediatrics_ Vol. 107, No. 2 (February).

Buckingham, David. 2003. _Media Education: Literacy, Learning and Contemporary Culture_. Malden, MA: Polity.

Dovey, J. 2001. "Reality TV." In G. Creeber (Ed.), _The Television Genre Book_ (134–137). London: British Film Institute.

Kaiser Family Foundation. 2005. "Generation M Media in the Lives of 8–18 Year-Old" (March).

Nielsen Media Research. 2005. "Nielsen Reports Americans Watch TV at Record Levels" (September). Available at: www.nielsenmedia.com

PBS Teacher Source. 1995–2006. "Media Literacy." Available at: www.pbs.org/teachersource/media_lit/media_lit.shtm (accessed April 2006).

Turn off the Violence. 2005. "Facts & Quotes." Available at: www.turnofftheviolence.org/facts&quotes.htm

VIDEOS

In the Mix: Media Literacy: TV—What You Don't See! Videocassette. PBS: Castleworks, 1997.

WEB SITES

Broadcasting and Cable: The Business of Television
www.broadcastingcable.com

Nielsen Media Research
www.nielsenmedia.com

Pew/Internet and American Life Project
www.pewinternet.org

6 MOVIES

"Films are an excellent source of authentic spoken language in context—a resource for both language and culture. This is especially true when it's American language and culture. Hollywood not only reflects American society; in some cases, it also creates it."

—Kitty Johnson, USIA English Teaching Fellow

"It can not be doubted that motion pictures are a significant medium for the communications of ideas. They may affect public attitudes and behavior in a variety of ways, ranging from direct espousal of a political or social doctrine to the subtle shaping of thought which characterizes all artistic expression. The importance of motion pictures as an organ of public opinion is not lessened by the fact that they are designed to entertain as well as to inform."

—U.S. Supreme Court in Burstyn v. Wilson

Motion pictures offer students endless hours of entertainment. How can we best use this form of entertainment in the classroom? This chapter will consider movies that fit with core areas, while focusing on understanding the techniques of editing, animation, and more. Please note that the words *movie* and *film* will be used interchangeably but refer to the same concept.

Film is a source of entertainment across the world. For teenagers, movies are a place where they can lose themselves and for which they are willing to spend a lot of time and money to attend. Bringing film to the classroom changes the linear approach to teaching, which at times is lecture and facts. Students can learn about the beginnings of film in the 1920s and the people who shaped it. More important, this class will leave the lecture style and require students to produce their own silent film, create appreciation for how much film has changed over the years, and at the same time offer awareness of the historical significance of this era.

Historically movies and films changed our society. As technology developed, the idea of a moving picture seemed rather evident. At the turn of the twentieth century, there were many people interested in the idea of the moving picture. One of the first to delve into this was Eadweard Muybridge. His concept of moving pictures was using photography to capture each change through photos. Muybridge is most famous for *Horse in Motion*, a mini-movie in which he set up multiple cameras at a race track in order to capture this idea of motion through the use of a horse racing. In many film schools, Muybridge is credited as being the father of film. Soon after, others became interested in the concept of movies, including Thomas Edison, who commandeered the market on films until the 1920s.

The first narrative film was *The Great Train Robbery*, also considered the first Western; however, all of the early films were silent. The 1920s brought about more technological advances including the introduction of sound, which both made and broke careers. Many actors and actresses who succeeded in silent film were unable to captivate their audiences when their voices were introduced.

The goals of this unit are as follows:

- To bring about another part of media literacy by showing how film has historically been an important part of our culture
- To create an understanding of the difficulties of immigrants and how the novelty of film changed their place in society
- To discuss the messages in film that led to the film code and the movie ratings systems
- To study the phenomenon of the movie star or celebrity by comparing the likes of Rudolph Valentino to current counterparts
- To understand why product placement in movies has changed the marketability of film on the big screen

The study of film is a natural outcome based upon the recommended curriculum elements supported by national and various state standards. It is important to note that the National Council for Teachers of English (NCTE), National Council for Social Studies (NCSS), and American Library Association (ALA) all promote curriculums in the area of film and motion pictures. Teaching about and through this topic can be easily incorporated into current standards and curriculums. This is also an opportunity for more media literacy core components to be incorporated into the current school model.

As the author of *Seeing and Believing*, Mary Christel, noted, "Many teachers feel that integrating a filmic text in a unit plan is a waste of time as it reflects popular culture which is usually synonymous with low culture. Let us keep in mind that many of the works of drama and fiction that are common to most English/Language Arts curricula at one time were part of a popular culture landscape; Shakespeare being a notable example. If film is analyzed with rigor and subtlety, it can reinforce and enrich that discussion of narrative and hopefully properties that are unique to a visual medium" (Christel and Krueger 2001).

Grade Level: These lessons have been primarily used in a classroom environment for grades five through eight; however, they are adaptable to all grade levels. You determine what best fits your classroom.

Curriculum Connections:	1. English—Reading, writing, and composition.
	2. Social Studies—Historical significance, Industrial Revolution, and various themes.
	3. Math—Product placement correlates with how companies are financially boosting their product line if it appears in a film.

4. Science—Inventions are the reason why film is a part of our society. Thomas Edison is one of the most famous names, but there were others.

Media Literacy Connections:

1. Media messages are constructed using a creative approach.

2. Different people experience the same media message differently.

3. Media are primarily businesses driven by a profit motive.

Time Frame:

These lessons can be used during a fifty-minute period. Keep in mind that sometimes the activity goes beyond the extended time period; therefore, plan accordingly. It is important to note that films or motion pictures are designed to be from two to three hours in length. Therefore, if you choose to show more than a few selected items, be prepared to extend lessons for two to three days. Lastly, there is no correct way to teach about a film or show a film. Some people prefer to show a film in its entirety and then discuss it with the class, while others prefer to stop a film in between. This is a classroom choice. As a library media specialist, your time is usually limited and it does not always behoove one to use that time to show an entire film. Make the decision based upon what you want to teach, how you want to teach it, and your own time constraints.

LESSON 6.1: HISTORY OF FILM AND THE MOTION PICTURE

Before You Begin

Much of the history of film blends with the U.S. History curriculums that we teach our students in middle and high school. They are intertwined, yet we teach very little of film, sound, music, or radio and their impact on our world. This particular lesson would fit well as a separate unit but can also be incorporated into the study of the Roaring Twenties, the Industrial Revolution, or inventions. This lesson covers the historical beginnings in a generalized way so that it fits middle schoolers, but it can be adapted and added to for high school students.

Objectives

- Students will be able to demonstrate some ways that radio, film, and TV changed the Americas' culture.
- Students will be provided with a working terminology of film and motion pictures.
- Students will comprehend the idea of "persistence of vision" through creating a flipbook and thaumatrope.
- Thaumatropes are small, round disks made out of hard cardboard with two holes popped in with strings attached. See Figure 6-1 and Supplement 6B for directions. You will need enough of these for the entire class and extras for students who will want to try more than one.
- Lastly, you will need enough directions for the class and colored pencils or markers for them to create their own designs.

Materials

- You will need a projecting system for a PowerPoint presentation on early film, available either in your classroom or at a computer lab.
- Prepare booklets that will work as a flipbook. Either these can be purchased or you can make them before the class begins. See Supplement 6A for directions.
- You will need enough copies for your class size of the flipbook and thaumatrope directions found in Supplements 6A and 6B.
- The following are items that will be needed in order to accomplish the two projects:
  - A pair of scissors
  - A needle and thread or something similar
  - A hole puncher
  - Colored pencils or markers

- • Small notebook, pad of paper, or nine-box sheet of paper
- • Stapler
- You will need an LCD projector, screen, and computer to display the PowerPoint presentation.

Process

- Begin the class by asking students:
  - • How are you able to see a film on the big screen?
  - • What technology is needed to make a film?
- Introduce the main term:
  - • Persistence of vision—A visual phenomenon where an image is retained in the eye for a short period of time, creating an illusion of continuous motion in film and video; usually understood to be twenty-four frames per second.
- Open up the PowerPoint presentation (Supplement 6C), and show only the first four slides. The PowerPoint has a brief history of early film along with clips of the first movies produced (these should be used with the following class).
- Demonstrate the class activity of flip books and thaumatropes using directions found in Supplements 6A and 6B.
- Once the flipbooks and thaumatropes are finished, have students share with the class their creations.

Assessment

Students will be assessed on how well they comprehend the term *persistence of vision* through their creations of a flipbook and thaumatrope. Students should also be assessed on their participation.

Reflection

This lesson may take up to two class periods. While the amount of material covered may seem minimal, the time students will take to demonstrate their understanding of persistence of vision is greater. Consider if you are short on time having students work together in pairs, which will also provide you with another opportunity for assessment.

Students tend to enjoy this class; the topic of film is one that they understand because they frequent and view them the most. Also, this is a lesson that gives students an opportunity to demonstrate their own creative abilities.

LESSON 6.2: THE IMMIGRANT CONNECTION

Before You Begin

Once again, this lesson fits well in conjunction with a social studies or U.S. History curriculum, which covers immigration at both the middle and high school levels. The theme of inventions is present in this lesson and therefore can be manipulated to work with a science lesson instead. The Power-Point includes four of the early inventors, but you may use others or just choose two or three as your focal point. You can easily download movie files on early film from the Internet. The accompanying CD-ROM includes the files for this lesson.

Objectives

1. Students will understand how the native culture of immigrants influenced American development.
2. Students will learn how early film changed America and how film progressed to the blockbusters of today.

Materials

- You will need enough copies for your size class of the film timeline, which can be found in Supplement 6C.
- You will need an LCD projector, screen, and computer to display the PowerPoint presentation.
- Note: Check to make sure that that your audio and viewing capabilities are ready prior to the class starting.

Process

- Begin class by asking students:
  - Who brought film to the big screen?
- Distribute to the class the film timeline (Supplement 6D).
- Ask students:
  - Who are immigrants?
  - What impact have they had on the production of film?

Ɪ the PowerPoint presentation (Supplement 6C),
ꞮInue with presentation beginning with Slide

Ɪɯ students some of the prominent early producers of film:

- Thomas Edison
- Lumière Brothers
- George Melies
- Eadweard Muybridge
- Edwin Porter

• As you introduce each major filmmaker, show samples of their work.

• Some of the short films to be screened:

- *The Great Train Robbery* by Edwin Porter
- *The Kiss* by Thomas Edison
- *A Trip to the Moon* by George Melies

• After each film, ask students to respond to what they are seeing. The reactions will be varied. Most will be surprised at how short movies were and at the low quality of films from before the 1920s.

• Ask students:

- Do they hear sound?
- What did they hear?

  • Answer: Sound was not introduced until the 1920s. Early film was silent. Usually, a piano player at the front of the theater accompanied the action found on the screen.

• Ask students:

- Would they enjoy film today without sound?
- What were some of the beneficial qualities of film without sound in the early part of the century?

  • Answer: The actors would have to be much more facially theatrical without the use of their voices.

- Would this work today?

• Close the class with a brief showing of a Charlie Chaplin film.

Assessment

Students will be assessed on their viewing and how they respond to the questions asked in class. This is an interactive exercise where the viewing is a portion and their reactions to what they are seeing are something else. Students should also be assessed on their participation and the quality of their responses.

Reflection

Early film can be amusing to the younger generation. It is important to point out that this was a primary phase of growth in the film industry and that film didn't even exist before this point. Bring this point closer to home by giving them an example of a tool they use today that was not in existence in the same way within their lifetime. An example of such a tool would be the Internet or even an iPod. This will help students to realize that technology and innovation has had a great impact on the kinds of items that they themselves use today.

LESSON 6.3: MOVIE STARS AND CELEBRITIES: YESTERDAY AND TODAY

Before You Begin

Celebrities were around before the beginnings of film, but film's wider range exposed actors to the world. Movie stars, whether male or female, have sometimes created followings that some would say verge on obsession. The paparazzi follow them, tabloids make stories of them, and they enter our homes every day through the news. Their movies have affected people to the point where followers, also known as celebrity gazers, want to know them or feel that they already do. This lesson provides students with a glimpse of how celebrities have become mainstream. It also shows them that celebrities also existed in the past.

Objectives

1. Students will understand the terms *celebrity*, *paparazzi*, and *tabloid*.
2. Students will recognize how a star is born into the mainstream media.
3. Students will write an informal letter to a celebrity of their choice.

- *Examiner*
- *National Enquirer*
- *Star*
- Magazines:
    - *Entertainment Weekly*
    - *People*
    - *Teen*
- Prior to the class, you will also need to find pictures of three or four early film movie stars. You will need to know a little background about each of the stars that you select. Here are a few to consider:
    - Charlie Chaplin
    - James Dean
    - Marilyn Monroe
    - Rudolph Valentino
- You will need a computer lab with a word processing program, Internet, and email capability.
- You will need letter-writing guidelines for each student.

Process

- Begin class by asking students to define the following terms:
    - Celebrity
    - Movie star
    - Paparazzi
    - Tabloid
- Introduce to students the early movie stars:
    - Rudolph Valentino—Known as "The Great Lover," he was considered the first true male movie sex symbol.

- James Dean—A cultural icon best known for being in teen angst situation films. His most acclaimed role was in the movie *Rebel Without a Cause*.
- Marilyn Monroe—A major pop icon of the twentieth century. She appeared in major feature films and was a big sex symbol.

- Ask students:
  - What made them such big celebrities?
  - How did people react to them?

- Pass out tabloids and magazines to students.
- Have students look at the cover and table of contents and flip through the magazine.
- Ask students:
  - Based on what they reviewed, who is considered a celebrity today?
  - Why do stars like Brad Pitt, Jennifer Aniston, and Lindsay Lohan capture the spotlight?

- Ask students to come up with their own list of celebrities.
  - Note: You may notice that many of the celebrities mentioned are crossovers from music to movies and vice-versa. This is not surprising, as many artists to day venture into different genres of media.

- Class activity:
  - Go to the computer lab.
  - Have students select a favorite celebrity.
  - Students should go onto the Internet and search for the celebrities' homepages. Most celebrities have one readily available.
  - Locate an email or a street address.
  - Their assignment is as follows:
    - Write the celebrity an email or letter.
    - Tell the celebrity how their work (name the title) somehow changed your way of thinking about yourself or the world around you. Make a connection between yourself and the celebrity or an event in the story. What questions would you have for this celebrity and what would you would like them to know?
    - Students should print their emails or word-processed letters.

- Close the class with some student sharings.

Assessment

Students should be assessed on their letter writing or email to celebrities. Therefore, specific guidelines for the letter writing exercise need to be given to students prior to their beginning their work, for example, clarity, conciseness, and how well informed they were about their celebrity of choice. Students will also be assessed on their participation and the quality of their responses.

Reflection

Many students of mine in the past were fortunate to receive responses to the letters written. Emailing is the quickest way to get a message to a celebrity, but the response tends to be one that has been mechanically set up as a response. Those students who wrote a letter via snail mail tended to receive a more direct response from their celebrity.

LESSON 6.4: FILM CODE AND MOVIE RATINGS

Before You Begin

Many students do not realize that a code for films and movies exists. Since the 1930s, the Hays Code, so named by its author William Hays, has been in place. The code took effect when people began reacting to films and found that some were indecent. These codes were a preliminary course of action in order to prevent filmmakers from producing films that were considered in bad taste. In the later part of the twentieth century, specifically, November 1, 1968, movie ratings were initiated. The ratings are determined by the Motion Picture Association of America and the National Association of Theatre Owners in order to help parents and other viewers with advance information on the content of films.

Objectives

1. Students will learn about the impact of the Hays Code on the movie industry.
2. Students will understand how movie ratings are decided and assigned to movies.

Materials

- Each student should receive a copy of the Hays Code found in Supplement 6E.
- A selection of scenes from a variety of movies should be in place to demonstrate some of the reasoning behind the Hays Code. For example, include a scene from any recent movie that showed a shooting or any other violent act. Once again, be very selective of the scenes that you show in class. Many PG-13 films today border on what would have fallen into the Hays Code categories.
- Provide students with a copy of the movie ratings guide found in Supplement 6F.

Process

- Begin class by asking students:
    - What kinds of movies are their favorites? Make a list by genre:
        - Horror
        - Mystery
        - Drama
        - Comedy
- Ask students:
    - How do they decide what is acceptable to watch at home? Who decides? What makes a movie acceptable or unacceptable?
    - Do they consider movies today decent or indecent?
        - Help students to define these terms as related to the movie industry.
    - Are movies too violent? Too vulgar?
- Pass out the Hays Code to students.
- Break students up into groups of four or five students.
    - Each group will be assigned one of the top four major categories to review and explain back to the class.
        - Crimes against the law
        - Sex
        - Vulgarity
        - Obscenity

- In their groups, ask students to discuss and come up with a plausible argument as to whether these codes would still be in effect today. Why or why not?
- Students must be prepared to report their findings and decisions back to the class.
- Students will be required to make a list of their talking points and submit them to the teacher.

- While students are working in groups, pass out the movie ratings sheet and their explanations as found in Supplement 6F.
- Ask students:

  - Compare the Hays Code with the current movie ratings.
  - Do they fit well, or are the items significantly different?

- Close class with group presentations on their findings.

Assessment

Students will be assessed on how well they work together in their groups investigating the Hays Code. The submission of each group's findings will also be a part of the assessment because it will verify what the students considered the most important aspects of the code and what they personally found to be insightful.

Reflection

This lesson is best suited for the high school student because of the content covered in the Hays Code. However, the lesson can be adapted to fit a middle school classroom by reviewing guidelines for movies and only portions of the Hays Code. As many of us know, our students are viewing programming that is far beyond their years. A number of parent groups have provided us with statistical documentation for how many violent acts are seen by children. This is not to say that all parents agree with the kinds of things their children see.

LESSON 6.5: PRODUCT PLACEMENT

Before You Begin

This is a lesson that will bring about a lot of conversation from your students and is fun, too! Filmmakers have found ways to pay for their films other than just in ticket sales. Product placement can be found in almost all of today's films, except for period pieces. What is product placement? Product placement is when a scene contains a product that looks like it should be there but has really been placed there to subconsciously get us to buy the product. For example, an actor or actress may drink a Diet Coke, happen to stop in at Starbucks for a coffee, or get a package delivered from Federal Express. While the items may seem like a natural part of the movie, the companies have paid for their products to be displayed throughout the film. It is a convenient and easy way for marketers to advertise their products. This lesson will show students how this is done.

Objectives

1. Students will understand the term *product placement*.
2. Students will be able to find products within a film easily that have been put there for the purpose of increasing marketing sales.

Materials

- A prepared ten- to fifteen-minute clip of a variety of movies that have products placed within the story.
- Select ten movies that would cover this topic and show one minute from each. Students can guess the movie and the product.
- Here are a list of a few movies where product placement was obvious:
    - *E.T.*
    - *You've Got Mail*
    - *Elf*
    - *Superman Returns*
    - *I, Robot*
- Students will need a sheet of paper and a pencil to document their information.
- You will also need a TV and VCR or DVD player.

Process

- Begin class by asking students:
    - Have they ever seen someone drinking a product, such as coffee or soda, in a movie?
    - Have they ever seen anyone eating food during a movie? Did anything stand out? Could they tell what company the food came from?

- Define the term *product placement*.
    - Discuss with students that this is a promotional tool used by marketers to influence their thinking subconsciously into buying a particular product.

- Class activity:
    - Tell students they are going to watch a ten- to fifteen-minute clip of a variety of movies.
    - Have students make a list from one to ten or for however many movies you have preselected.
    - Tell students to write down the product that they saw and also try to guess the movie that it was placed in.
    - Tell students they must be prepared to discuss the results of their findings after the showing.

- Discuss with the class the products they listed and reveal the names of the movies.

- Ask students:
    - Were they surprised at the number of products found in movies?
    - Will they be aware of them the next time they watch a movie?
    - Do they think product placement works?
        - *Possible Answer:* Some students will be able to tell you right away that they were hungry or thirsty for something they had just seen, thus demonstrating what marketers already know to be true: Product placement works.

- Close class with a student reflection.
    - Students can note what they learned in the class and their reactions to the idea of product placement.

Assessment

Assess students on how they respond to the questions asked in class. Also assess them on their participation in the class activities and the quality of their responses.

Reflection

Students are always fascinated with how marketers are able to entice them to buy a product. This exercise is one of the simplest ways to show how this is done so effectively. More important, it teaches students the media literacy lesson that all media messages are constructed. In this case, the construction is to promote the buying power of certain products sold during the viewing of a film.

SUPPLEMENT 6A: FLIPBOOK DIRECTIONS

A flipbook is like a cartoon. Each page has a picture slightly different from the picture before it so that when the pages of the book are flipped it looks like the pictures are moving.

You will need:

- Small notebook, pad of paper, or nine-box sheet of paper
- Colored pencils or markers
- Stapler

Directions:

- Choose a simple action to show with your flipbook. Examples include a face changing from sad to happy, a person walking, or an apple falling from a tree.
- On the last page of the flipbook, draw the first picture in the action sequence (for example, the sad face).
- On the next-to-last page, draw the same picture but with a slight change (for example, the frown lifting a bit).
- Draw each subsequent picture so it's slightly different from the one before it until the action sequence is complete.
- Flip through the pages to see the animation.

Figure 6-1. Flipbook

Note: You may also want to distribute a sheet of paper with nine boxes similar to those above. Students can draw on them, cut them in the order of their pictures, and then staple them together on the side.

SUPPLEMENT 6B: THAUMATROPE DIRECTIONS

The thaumatrope was an animation toy from the early 1900s to demonstrate the concept of persistence of vision. Use the template below to make your own thaumatrope.

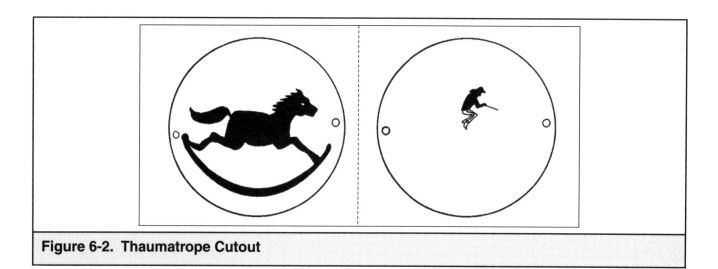

Figure 6-2. Thaumatrope Cutout

You will need:

- A pair of scissors
- A needle and thread or something similar
- A hole puncher
- Colored pencils or markers

Directions:

- Cut out the large rectangle.
- Fold along the line. Hold the paper up to the light to be sure the circles line up.
- Put some glue on the back of the circles and stick them together.
- Cut out the circle. Use a pencil or hole punch to make small holes where each of the black dots is marked.
- Use a needle and thread to tie a short string to each of the holes on the sides of the circle.
- Rub the strings between your fingers to twirl the thaumatrope.

Now use the following blank templates to create your own creative thaumatropes.

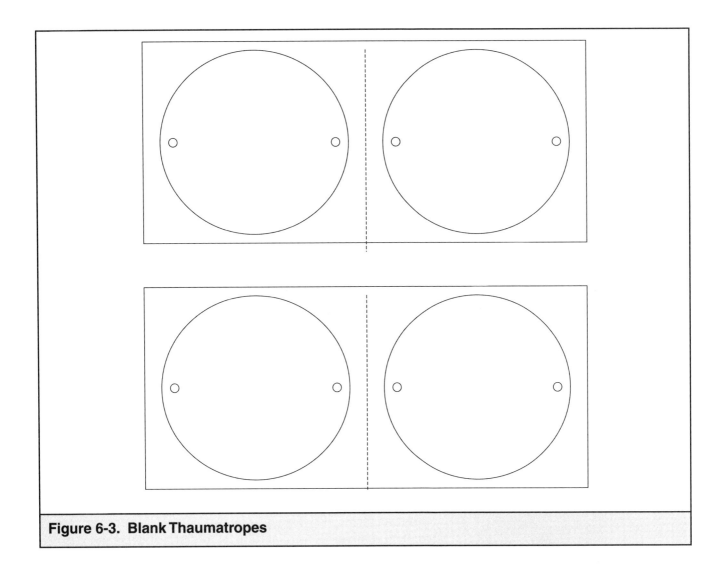

Figure 6-3. Blank Thaumatropes

SUPPLEMENT 6C: FILM TIMELINE: 1800s TO 1930s

1877—Eadweard Muybridge synchronizes twenty-four cameras to photograph horses galloping. When the photos are placed in order and rotated, it looks like the horse in the photos is galloping.

1886–1914—Magician George Melies invents trick photography and begins incorporating it into film. He creates over a thousand short films including *A Trip to the Moon* in 1902.

1894—The Edison Corporation establishes the first motion-picture studio, a Kinetograph production center nicknamed the Black María (slang for a police van). The first Kinetoscope parlor opens at 1155 Broadway in New York City. Spectators can watch films for twenty-five cents.

1895—In France, Auguste and Louis Lumière hold the first private screening. The brothers invent the *cinématographe*, a combination camera and projector. The image of an oncoming train is said to have caused an audience stampede.

1903—Edison Corporation mechanic Edwin S. Porter turns cameraman, director, and producer to make *The Great Train Robbery*. With fourteen shots cutting between simultaneous events, this twelve-minute short establishes the shot as film's basic element and editing as a central narrative device. It is also the first Western.

1905—The first movie theater opens in Pittsburgh.

1910—Thomas Edison introduces his kinetophone, which makes talkies a reality.

1914—In his second big-screen appearance, Charlie Chaplin plays the Little Tramp, his most famous character.

1916—Charlie Chaplin signs on with Mutual Studios and earns an unprecedented $10,000 a week.

1919—Charlie Chaplin, D. W. Griffith, Douglas Fairbanks, and Mary Pickford establish United Artists in an attempt to control their own work.

1921—*The Sheik*, directed by George Melford, debuts and establishes star Rudolph Valentino as cinema's best-known lover.

1924—Walt Disney creates his first cartoon, *Alice's Wonderland*.

1925—*Ben-Hur*, costing a record-setting $3.95 million to produce, is released.

1928—Walt Disney introduces *Galloping Gaucho* and *Steamboat Willie*, the first cartoons with sound. The Academy Awards are handed out for the first time. *Wings* wins Best Picture.

SUPPLEMENT 6D: MOTION PICTURE TERMINOLOGY

Blockbuster: Movie which is a huge financial success, making $100 million or more.

Cinematographer: The movie photographer responsible for camera technique and lighting during production.

Director: The person in charge of the overall look of a video or film produced. The director directs the action behind and in front of the camera.

Documentary: A film or video that explores a subject in such a way that the information appears to be factual and accurate.

Persistence of vision: A visual phenomenon where an image is retained in the eye for a short period of time, creating an illusion of continuous motion in film and video; usually understood to be twenty-four frames per second.

Producer: The final authority in the electronic media production process. Sometimes the producer is the person who raises the money to produce media products.

Scene: A series of shots that conveys a unified element of a movie's story.

Sound effects: Sounds used to suggest a story element such as background, time, place, or character. Also used to heighten and intensify action or evoke an emotional response.

Trailer: A short filmed preview or advertisement for a movie.

SUPPLEMENT 6E: HAYS CODE

As head of the Motion Picture Producers and Distributors of America, William Hays established a code of decency (presented here courtesy of the Motion Picture Association of America) that outlines what is acceptable in films (1930).

If motion pictures present stories that will affect lives for the better, they can become the most powerful force for the improvement of mankind.

A Code to Govern the Making of Talking, Synchronized and Silent Motion Pictures. Formulated and formally adopted by The Association of Motion Picture Producers, Inc. and The Motion Picture Producers and Distributors of America, Inc. in March 1930.

Motion picture producers recognize the high trust and confidence which have been placed in them by the people of the world and which have made motion pictures a universal form of entertainment.

They recognize their responsibility to the public because of this trust and because entertainment and art are important influences in the life of a nation.

Hence, though regarding motion pictures primarily as entertainment without any explicit purpose of teaching or propaganda, they know that the motion picture within its own field of entertainment may be directly responsible for spiritual or moral progress, for higher types of social life, and for much correct thinking.

During the rapid transition from silent to talking pictures they have realized the necessity and the opportunity of subscribing to a Code to govern the production of talking pictures and of re-acknowledging this responsibility.

On their part, they ask from the public and from public leaders a sympathetic understanding of their purposes and problems and a spirit of cooperation that will allow them the freedom and opportunity necessary to bring the motion picture to a still higher level of wholesome entertainment for all the people.

GENERAL PRINCIPLES

1. No picture shall be produced that will lower the moral standards of those who see it. Hence the sympathy of the audience should never be thrown to the side of crime, wrongdoing, evil or sin.
2. Correct standards of life, subject only to the requirements of drama and entertainment, shall be presented.
3. Law, natural or human, shall not be ridiculed, nor shall sympathy be created for its violation.

PARTICULAR APPLICATIONS

I. Crimes Against the Law

These shall never be presented in such a way as to throw sympathy with the crime as against law and justice or to inspire others with a desire for imitation.

1. Murder
   a. The technique of murder must be presented in a way that will not inspire imitation.
   b. Brutal killings are not to be presented in detail.
   c. Revenge in modern times shall not be justified.
2. Methods of Crime should not be explicitly presented.
   a. Theft, robbery, safe-cracking, and dynamiting of trains, mines, buildings, etc., should not be detailed in method.
   b. Arson must subject to the same safeguards.
   c. The use of firearms should be restricted to the essentials.
   d. Methods of smuggling should not be presented.
3. Illegal drug traffic must never be presented.

4. The use of liquor in American life, when not required by the plot or for proper characterization, will not be shown.

II. Sex

The sanctity of the institution of marriage and the home shall be upheld. Pictures shall not infer that low forms of sex relationship are the accepted or common thing.

1. Adultery, sometimes necessary plot material, must not be explicitly treated, or justified, or presented attractively.

2. Scenes of Passion

   a. They should not be introduced when not essential to the plot.

   b. Excessive and lustful kissing, lustful embraces, suggestive postures and gestures, are not to be shown.

   c. In general passion should so be treated that these scenes do not stimulate the lower and baser element.

3. Seduction or Rape

   a. They should never be more than suggested, and only when essential for the plot, and even then never shown by explicit method.

   b. They are never the proper subject for comedy.

4. Sex perversion or any inference to it is forbidden.

5. White slavery shall not be treated.

6. Miscegenation (sex relationships between the white and black races) is forbidden.

7. Sex hygiene and venereal diseases are not subjects for motion pictures.

8. Scenes of actual child birth, in fact or in silhouette, are never to be presented.

9. Children's sex organs are never to be exposed.

III. Vulgarity

The treatment of low, disgusting, unpleasant, though not necessarily evil, subjects should always be subject to the dictates of good taste and a regard for the sensibilities of the audience.

IV. Obscenity

Obscenity in word, gesture, reference, song, joke, or by suggestion (even when likely to be understood only by part of the audience) is forbidden.

V. Profanity

Pointed profanity (this includes the words, God, Lord, Jesus, Christ—unless used reverently—Hell, S.O.B., damn, Gawd), or every other profane or vulgar expression however used, is forbidden.

VI. Costume

1. Complete nudity is never permitted. This includes nudity in fact or in silhouette, or any lecherous or licentious notice thereof by other characters in the picture.
2. Undressing scenes should be avoided, and never used save where essential to the plot.
3. Indecent or undue exposure is forbidden.
4. Dancing or costumes intended to permit undue exposure or indecent movements in the dance are forbidden.

VII. Dances

1. Dances suggesting or representing sexual actions or indecent passions are forbidden.
2. Dances which emphasize indecent movements are to be regarded as obscene.

VIII. Religion

1. No film or episode may throw ridicule on any religious faith.
2. Ministers of religion in their character as ministers of religion should not be used as comic characters or as villains.
3. Ceremonies of any definite religion should be carefully and respectfully handled.

IX. Locations

The treatment of bedrooms must be governed by good taste and delicacy.

X. National Feelings

1. The use of the Flag shall be consistently respectful.
2. The history, institutions, prominent people and citizenry of other nations shall be represented fairly.

XI. Titles

Salacious, indecent, or obscene titles shall not be used.

XII. Repellent Subjects

The following subjects must be treated within the careful limits of good taste:

1. Actual hangings or electrocutions as legal punishments for crime.
2. Third degree methods.
3. Brutality and possible gruesomeness.
4. Branding of people or animals.
5. Apparent cruelty to children or animals.
6. The sale of women, or a woman selling her virtue.
7. Surgical operations.

REASONS SUPPORTING THE PREAMBLE OF THE CODE

I. Theatrical motion pictures, that is, pictures intended for the theatre as distinct from pictures intended for churches, schools, lecture halls, educational movements, social reform movements, etc., are primarily to be regarded as ENTERTAINMENT.

Mankind has always recognized the importance of entertainment and its value in rebuilding the bodies and souls of human beings.

But it has always recognized that entertainment can be a character either HELPFUL or HARMFUL to the human race, and in consequence has clearly distinguished between:

a. Entertainment which tends to improve the race, or at least to re-create and rebuild human beings exhausted with the realities of life; and

b. Entertainment which tends to degrade human beings, or to lower their standards of life and living.

Hence the MORAL IMPORTANCE of entertainment is something which has been universally recognized. It enters intimately into the lives of men and women and affects them closely; it occupies their minds and affections during leisure hours; and ultimately touches the whole of their lives. A man may be judged by his standard of entertainment as easily as by the standard of his work.

So correct entertainment raises the whole standard of a nation.

Wrong entertainment lowers the whole living conditions and moral ideals of a race.

Note, for example, the healthy reactions to healthful sports, like baseball, golf; the unhealthy reactions to sports like cockfighting, bullfighting, bear baiting, etc.

Note, too, the effect on ancient nations of gladiatorial combats, the obscene plays of Roman times, etc.

II. Motion pictures are very important as art.

Though a new art, possibly a combination art, it has the same object as the other arts, the presentation of human thought, emotion, and experience, in terms of an appeal to the soul through the senses.

Here, as in entertainment,

Art enters intimately into the lives of human beings.

Art can be morally good, lifting men to higher levels. This has been done through good music, great painting, authentic fiction, poetry, drama.

Art can be morally evil in its effects. This is the case clearly enough with unclean art, indecent books, suggestive drama. The effect on the lives of men and women are obvious.

Note: It has often been argued that art itself is unmoral, neither good nor bad. This is true of the THING which is music, painting, poetry, etc. But the THING is the PRODUCT of some person's mind, and the intention of that mind was either good or bad morally when it produced the thing. Besides, the thing has its EFFECT upon those who come into contact with it. In both these ways, that is, as a product of a mind and as the cause of definite effects, it has a deep moral significance and unmistakable moral quality.

Hence: The motion pictures, which are the most popular of modern arts for the masses, have their moral quality from the intention of the minds which produce them and from their effects on the moral lives and reactions of their audiences. This gives them a most important morality.

1. They reproduce the morality of the men who use the pictures as a medium for the expression of their ideas and ideals.

2. They affect the moral standards of those who, through the screen, take in these ideas and ideals.

In the case of motion pictures, the effect may be particularly emphasized because no art has so quick and so widespread an appeal to the masses. It has become in an incredibly short period the art of the multitudes.

III. The motion picture, because of its importance as entertainment and because of the trust placed in it by the peoples of the world, has special moral obligations:

    A. Most arts appeal to the mature. This art appeals at once to every class, mature, immature, developed, undeveloped, law abiding, criminal. Music has its grades for different classes; so has literature and drama. This art of the motion picture, combining as it does the two fundamental appeals of looking at a picture and listening to a story, at once reaches every class of society.

    B. By reason of the mobility of film and the ease of picture distribution, and because the possibility of duplicating positives in large quantities, this art reaches places unpenetrated by other forms of art.

    C. Because of these two facts, it is difficult to produce films intended for only certain classes of people. The exhibitors' theatres are built for the masses, for the cultivated and the rude, the mature and the immature, the self-respecting and the criminal. Films, unlike books and music, can with difficulty be confined to certain selected groups.

    D. The latitude given to film material cannot, in consequence, be as wide as the latitude given to book material. In addition:

        a. A book describes; a film vividly presents. One presents on a cold page; the other by apparently living people.

        b. A book reaches the mind through words merely; a film reaches the eyes and ears through the reproduction of actual events.

        c. The reaction of a reader to a book depends largely on the keenness of the reader's imagination; the reaction to a film depends on the vividness of presentation.

Hence many things which might be described or suggested in a book could not possibly be presented in a film.

    E. This is also true when comparing the film with the newspaper.

        a. Newspapers present by description, films by actual presentation.

        b. Newspapers are after the fact and present things as having taken place; the film gives the events in the process of enactment and with apparent reality of life.

F. Everything possible in a play is not possible in a film:

   a. Because of the larger audience of the film, and its consequential mixed character. Psychologically, the larger the audience, the lower the moral mass resistance to suggestion.

   b. Because through light, enlargement of character, presentation, scenic emphasis, etc., the screen story is brought closer to the audience than the play.

   c. The enthusiasm for and interest in the film actors and actresses, developed beyond anything of the sort in history, makes the audience largely sympathetic toward the characters they portray and the stories in which they figure. Hence the audience is more ready to confuse actor and actress and the characters they portray, and it is most receptive of the emotions and ideals presented by the favorite stars.

G. Small communities, remote from sophistication and from the hardening process which often takes place in the ethical and moral standards of larger cities, are easily and readily reached by any sort of film.

H. The grandeur of mass settings, large action, spectacular features, etc., affects and arouses more intensely the emotional side of the audience.

In general, the mobility, popularity, accessibility, emotional appeal, vividness, and straightforward presentation of fact in the film make for more intimate contact with a larger audience and for greater emotional appeal.

Hence the larger moral responsibilities of the motion pictures.

REASONS UNDERLYING THE GENERAL PRINCIPLES

I. No picture shall be produced which will lower the moral standards of those who see it.

Hence the sympathy of the audience should never be thrown to the side of crime, wrong-doing, evil or sin.
This is done:

   1. When evil is made to appear attractive and alluring, and good is made to appear unattractive.

2. When the sympathy of the audience is thrown on the side of crime, wrongdoing, evil, sin. The same is true of a film that would throw sympathy against goodness, honor, innocence, purity or honesty.

Note: Sympathy with a person who sins is not the same as sympathy with the sin or crime of which he is guilty. We may feel sorry for the plight of the murderer or even understand the circumstances which led him to his crime: we may not feel sympathy with the wrong which he has done. The presentation of evil is often essential for art or fiction or drama. This in itself is not wrong provided:

A. That evil is not presented alluringly. Even if later in the film the evil is condemned or punished, it must not be allowed to appear so attractive that the audience's emotions are drawn to desire or approve so strongly that later the condemnation is forgotten and only the apparent joy of sin is remembered.

B. That throughout, the audience feels sure that evil is wrong and good is right.

II. Correct standards of life shall, as far as possible, be presented.

A wide knowledge of life and of living is made possible through the film. When right standards are consistently presented, the motion picture exercises the most powerful influences. It builds character, develops right ideals, inculcates correct principles, and all this in attractive story form.

If motion pictures consistently hold up for admiration high types of characters and present stories that will affect lives for the better, they can become the most powerful force for the improvement of mankind.

III. Law, natural or human, shall not be ridiculed, nor shall sympathy be created for its violation.

By natural law is understood the law which is written in the hearts of all mankind, the greater underlying principles of right and justice dictated by conscience.

By human law is understood the law written by civilized nations.

1. The presentation of crimes against the law is often necessary for the carrying out of the plot. But the presentation must not throw sympathy with the crime as against the law nor with the criminal as against those who punish him.

2. The courts of the land should not be presented as unjust. This does not mean that a single court may not be presented as unjust, much less that a single court official must not be presented this way. But the court

system of the country must not suffer as a result of this presentation.

REASONS UNDERLYING THE PARTICULAR APPLICATIONS

I. Sin and evil enter into the story of human beings and hence in themselves are valid dramatic material.

II. In the use of this material, it must be distinguished between sin which repels by its very nature, and sins which often attract.

    A. In the first class come murder, most theft, many legal crimes, lying, hypocrisy, cruelty, etc.

    B. In the second class come sex sins, sins and crimes of apparent heroism, such as banditry, daring thefts, leadership in evil, organized crime, revenge, etc.

The first class needs less care in treatment, as sins and crimes of this class are naturally unattractive. The audience instinctively condemns all such and is repelled.

Hence the important objective must be to avoid the hardening of the audience, especially of those who are young and impressionable, to the thought and fact of crime. People can become accustomed even to murder, cruelty, brutality, and repellent crimes, if these are too frequently repeated.

The second class needs great care in handling, as the response of human nature to their appeal is obvious. This is treated more fully below.

III. A careful distinction can be made between films intended for general distribution, and films intended for use in theatres restricted to a limited audience.

Themes and plots quite appropriate for the latter would be altogether out of place and dangerous in the former.

Note: The practice of using a general theatre and limiting its patronage to "Adults Only" is not completely satisfactory and is only partially effective.

However, maturer minds may easily understand and accept without harm subject matter in plots which do younger people positive harm.

Hence: If there should be created a special type of theatre, catering exclusively to an adult audience, for plays of this character (plays with problem themes, difficult discussions and maturer treatment) it would seem to afford an outlet, which does not now exist, for pictures unsuitable for general distribution but permissible for exhibitions to a restricted audience.

I. Crimes Against the Law

The treatment of crimes against the law must not:

1. Teach methods of crime.
2. Inspire potential criminals with a desire for imitation.
3. Make criminals seem heroic and justified.

Revenge in modern times shall not be justified. In lands and ages of less developed civilization and moral principles, revenge may sometimes be presented. This would be the case especially in places where no law exists to cover the crime because of which revenge is committed.

Because of its evil consequences, the drug traffic should not be presented in any form. The existence of the trade should not be brought to the attention of audiences.

The use of liquor should never be excessively presented. In scenes from American life, the necessities of plot and proper characterization alone justify its use. And in this case, it should be shown with moderation.

II. Sex

Out of a regard for the sanctity of marriage and the home, the triangle, that is, the love of a third party for one already married, needs careful handling. The treatment should not throw sympathy against marriage as an institution.

Scenes of passion must be treated with an honest acknowledgement of human nature and its normal reactions. Many scenes cannot be presented without arousing dangerous emotions on the part of the immature, the young or the criminal classes.

Even within the limits of pure love, certain facts have been universally regarded by lawmakers as outside the limits of safe presentation.

In the case of impure love, the love which society has always regarded as wrong and which has been banned by divine law, the following are important:

1. Impure love must not be presented as attractive and beautiful.
2. It must not be the subject of comedy or farce, or treated as material for laughter.
3. It must not be presented in such a way to arouse passion or morbid curiosity on the part of the audience.
4. It must not be made to seem right and permissible.
5. In general, it must not be detailed in method and manner.

III. Vulgarity; IV. Obscenity; V. Profanity;

hardly need further explanation than is contained in the Code.

VI. Costume

General Principles:

1. The effect of nudity or semi-nudity upon the normal man or woman, and much more upon the young and upon immature persons, has been honestly recognized by all lawmakers and moralists.
2. Hence the fact that the nude or semi-nude body may be beautiful does not make its use in the films moral. For, in addition to its beauty, the effect of the nude or semi-nude body on the normal individual must be taken into consideration.
3. Nudity or semi-nudity used simply to put a "punch" into a picture comes under the head of immoral actions. It is immoral in its effect on the average audience.
4. Nudity can never be permitted as being necessary for the plot. Semi-nudity must not result in undue or indecent exposures.
5. Transparent or translucent materials and silhouette are frequently more suggestive than actual exposure.

VII. Dances

Dancing in general is recognized as an art and as a beautiful form of expressing human emotions.

But dances which suggest or represent sexual actions, whether performed solo or with two or more; dances intended to excite the emotional reaction of an audience; dances with movement of the breasts, excessive body movements while the feet are stationary, violate decency and are wrong.

VIII. Religion

The reason why ministers of religion may not be comic characters or villains is simply because the attitude taken toward them may easily become the attitude taken toward religion in general. Religion is lowered in the minds of the audience because of the lowering of the audience's respect for a minister.

IX. Locations

Certain places are so closely and thoroughly associated with sexual life or with sexual sin that their use must be carefully limited.

X. National Feelings

The just rights, history, and feelings of any nation are entitled to most careful consideration and respectful treatment.

XI. Titles

As the title of a picture is the brand on that particular type of goods, it must conform to the ethical practices of all such honest business.

XII. Repellent Subjects

Such subjects are occasionally necessary for the plot. Their treatment must never offend good taste nor injure the sensibilities of an audience.

SUPPLEMENT 6F: MOVIE RATINGS GUIDE

G: General Audience. All ages admitted. This signifies that the film rated contains nothing most parents will consider offensive for even their youngest children to see or hear. Nudity, sex scenes, and scenes of drug use are absent; violence is minimal; snippets of dialogue may go beyond polite conversation but do not go beyond common everyday expressions.

PG: Parental Guidance Suggested. Some material may not be suitable for children. This signifies that the film rated may contain some material parents might not like to expose to their young children—material that will clearly need to be examined or inquired about before children are allowed to attend the film. Explicit sex scenes and scenes of drug use are absent; nudity, if present, is seen only briefly; horror and violence do not exceed moderate levels.

PG-13: Parents Strongly Cautioned. Some material may be inappropriate for children under 13. This signifies that the film rated may be inappropriate for preteens. Parents should be especially careful about letting their younger children attend. Rough or persistent violence is absent; sexually oriented nudity is generally absent; some scenes of drug use may be seen; one use of the harsher sexually derived words may be heard.

R: Restricted—Under 17. Requires accompanying parent or adult guardian (age varies in some locations). This signifies that the rating board has concluded that the film rated contains some adult material. Parents are urged to learn more about the film before taking their children to see it. An R may be assigned due to, among other things, a film's use of language, theme, violence, or sex or its portrayal of drug use.

NC-17: No One 17 and Under Admitted. This signifies that the rating board believes that most American parents would feel that the film is patently adult and that children age 17 and under should not be admitted to it. The film may contain explicit sex scenes, an accumulation of sexually oriented language, or scenes of excessive violence. The NC-17 designation does not, however, signify that the rated film is obscene or pornographic.

—Motion Picture Association of America

REFERENCES

BOOKS

Christel, Mary T., and Ellen Krueger. 2001. *Seeing and Believing: How to Teach Media Literacy in the English Classroom.* New York: Boynton/Cook.

Monaco, James. 2000. *How to Read a Film*, 3rd ed. New York: Oxford Press.

Platt, Richard. 1992. *Film.* New York: Dorling Kindersley.

Richards, Andrea. 2005. *Girl Director: A How-To Guide for the First-Time Flat Broke Film and Video Maker.* Berkeley, CA: Ten Speed Press.

Wordsworth, Louise. 1999. *Film and Television.* Austin, TX: Raintree Steck-Vaughn.

VIDEOS

History of the 20th Century. Videocassette. MPI Home Video, 2001.

The Movies Begin, Vols. 1–5. DVD. New York: Kino International, 2002.

WEB SITES

Internet Movie Database
www.imdb.com

Super-8 Filmmaking: Film Stocks
www.super8filmmaking.com

Teach with Movies
www.teachwithmovies.org

YALSA—Young Adult Library Services Association's Internet Guide for
Teens
www.ala./teenhoopla/motives.html

7 PHOTOGRAPHY AND IMAGES

"Photography, as a powerful medium of expression and communications, offers an infinite variety of perception, interpretation and execution."

—*Ansel Adams*

People taking photographs often say, "Say cheese!" and "Smile!" Usually, the photographer is capturing people, places, or special events. A picture is worth a thousand words personally, politically, and societally. Photographs equal memories or moments in time captured to engage an audience.

In today's media-filled environment, the photograph is used for many purposes, including deception, documentation, newsworthiness, and propaganda. Some of the most famous photographs have detailed world events such as the Vietnam War, Columbine, and September 11. Pictures speak to our emotions. We instinctively react to what we see. Pictures show us pain, fear, love, happiness, and grief. Certainly, the media use these feelings in order to promote a message. For example, we are shown images of war that are graphic and detailed or less graphic images that appeal to patriotism. Politicians are often photographed holding a child or shaking a poor man's hand. Those photographs have ulterior motives. Photos encourage us to think a certain way about a person or an event.

Photographs are open to a variety of interpretations. An image printed in a news magazine serves to tell a factual event or to convince the viewer that an event took place. Each person who sees the photo interprets what they see based upon their prior knowledge of an event and their background.

Photography has been around since the nineteenth century. From the beginning photos were taken with a purpose in mind, such as to document historical events or to capture newsworthy events. As time has passed the purpose of photographs has evolved. Today, they may create controversy, change real-life events, and even in some cases completely retell a story inaccurately. This media format presents a variety of viewpoints while communicating news and information. Photos are able to capture a bias, proclaim someone guilty, or even make an event look worse than it really is. Recently, photos have become a source of contention. Computer programs such as Adobe Photoshop are now used in news agencies, magazine editing houses, and even people's homes. These programs make it easier to eliminate or add items to photographs, thereby changing the context or the message presented. This creates questions of whether a photo is real or whether it has been manipulated. What does photo manipulation actually mean? What do extremely cropped photos leave out? What has been changed about a time or place captured on film? Modern technologies make detecting truth versus fiction more complicated. New photographic technologies have also created concerns in the news industry. Is the photograph airbrushed or does the model really look that good? Is that really Bill Clinton hugging Monica Lewinsky or was her image dropped into the picture using Photoshop? Are the war photographs we are seeing real or are they created images?

The lessons in this chapter teach students about photo appreciation while also looking at some of the negative and positive aspects of photo manipulation. The last lesson asks students to look at Pulitzer Prize photos. The Pulitzer Prize photos demonstrate why photographs should remain in their original form so that viewers can understand their historical significance and newsworthiness.

My fascination with Pulitzer Prize photos began four years ago when I visited the Freedom Forum in New York City. The Freedom Forum was having a celebratory program for the Pulitzer and had the photographs, along with the photographers' stories, blown up to life-size proportions and displayed. The experience was like walking through moments of history while experiencing joy, pain, suffering, war, love, and peace. The photographs in that particular size were impressive and intense. My goal was to try to duplicate that type of intensity in the classroom while discussing the importance of photographs such as these in comparison to ones that have been changed to conform to an idea decided by an editor.

The first time I taught this lesson demonstrated the significance of visual images and their influence on youth. When the students walked into the room and saw the Pulitzer Prize photos, they were instantly enthralled. The room fell silent immediately as they walked around looking and reading. They would pull their classmates over to share a photograph and their thoughts. It was an amazing experience for me as an educator. It was a simple activity, but it did so much for their understanding of how photographs make deep impressions.

There are several practical purposes for the use of photographs in different subject areas. Media specialists have access to a variety of different teachers in these specialty areas and a variety of materials; therefore, the potential for this exercise is limitless. Photos can be used on their own, but they have greater use when their meaning matches what is going on in a curriculum area.

In the Language Arts/English classroom, photographs can be used to inspire an investigation of visual texts and their purpose in society. Teachers can use photography to talk about messages or content, or even use the theme of "a picture is worth a thousand words" as a method for discussing language, voice, theme, and point of view. In a history classroom, pictures can spark discussions of propaganda, political motivations, and stereotyping. Certainly, pictures are a connection to the past. They explain events in history, they reflect the passing of time, and they open doorways to change.

Pictures can also be considered an art form. You may use this lesson on the meaning of photographs and then ask students to snap pictures and use them in projects, as a creative outlet, or to tell a personal story. These are just a few examples of what lessons on photography can offer to students and teachers.

In this chapter, you will find a series of lessons that develop the ideas of photography and the importance of critical thinking skills.

Grade Level: These lessons have been primarily used in a classroom environment for grades five through eight; however, they are adaptable to all grade levels. You determine what best fits your classroom.

Curriculum Connections:	1. English—Reading, writing, and composition.
	2. Social Studies—A variety of connections based on content of photos selected.
Media Literacy Connections:	1. All media messages are constructed.
	2. Media have embedded values and points of view.
Time Frame:	These lessons can be used in a fifty-minute period. Keep in mind that sometimes the activity goes beyond the extended time period; therefore, plan accordingly.

LESSON 7.1: BASIC PHOTO APPRECIATION

Before You Begin

This introductory lesson in photography asks students to examine what they know about photographs and to understand the meaning they play in our society. Ask students to bring two to three pictures that are of personal significance to them such as family or friend pictures or snapshots. You should also have some to share with the class so that they can make the connection that photographs reach everyone, whatever their age, ethnicity, or lifestyle.

Objectives

1. Students will develop an awareness of photography through visual literacy.
2. Students will understand basic photography terms.
3. Students will appreciate aesthetically a good quality photograph and understand its societal importance.

Materials

- Students and instructor should bring to the classroom two to three photographs of their choosing.

Process

- Ask the class:

    - What is a photograph and what importance do photographs have in our society?
    - How are photographs used in their families? Where else are photos popular?

- Ask students why photographs having meaning to them. This will bring about a lot of discussion including the kind of cameras they use, whether digital, instamatic, or 35mm film.
- Introduce the terms that students will be encountering during their lessons on photography. See Supplement 7A.
- Introduce the photos that you brought to the classroom. Discuss their meaning to you and why they were taken.
- Break students up into pairs and allow five to ten minutes for discussion of the photographs that they brought in to share.
- Ask students:

    - Who took the picture?
    - Is there anything wrong with the picture aesthetically?
    - If you could change the picture, what would be different?

- Select five students to come to the front of the class and share their photos and their insights on them.
- Close the class by reminding students that photographs have been a part of our history and have made impressions on generations of people, just as their photographs have for their families.

Assessment

Students can be assessed based on participation and the quality of their insights.

Reflection

One of the greatest outcomes of teaching about photographs is seeing how individually we react to them. In most cases, what we see affects us, either because we know the people in the photographs or because the event pictured has some significance. Even the photos we realize that were taken badly cause some reaction—maybe a laugh or perhaps even disgust. This preliminary exercise gives the classroom teacher an opportunity to see what students value based on their choice of photos.

This is a good time to discuss students' choices and respecting those choices. When students contribute in any classroom situation there is trepidation because their input will be either accepted or rejected. Photographs that are of personal relevance to students may be especially sensitive. Tell students that the photos they bring to class should be appropriate to the environment. It will save you and your students any kind of grief that could potentially result.

LESSON 7.2: CAPTIONING PHOTOGRAPHS

Before You Begin

There are two parts to this lesson, so it may extend to a second class. The point of this lesson is get students engaged in photographs and the stories they tell. The Web site provided has an enormous photo gallery, which contains news, historical, and entertainment photos.

Objectives

1. Students will learn to relate captions to photographs.
2. Students will learn to write captions for photographs.

PART 1: REVIEWING PHOTOS WITH CAPTIONS

Materials

- Provide the class with the daily newspaper. Most newspaper companies will provide for schools, free of charge, a classroom set for use with a unit of study. Many newspapers also have educational programs that tie in with classroom activities. You can find more information about this through the *Newspapers in Education* Web site: http://nieonline.com/. This Web site provides many lessons and further activities related to newspapers and visual and media literacy. As with any other lesson, remember to plan ahead and contact your local newspaper so that your materials will be ready for use. If for some reason your local paper is not a part of this educational program, have each student bring a newspaper to class.

- This portion of the lesson also requires a computer lab with an Internet connection. If a computer lab is not possible for a class, instructors may choose to print out multiple copies of each photograph prior to the lesson. These printouts can then be distributed to students at their desks.

Web Site

The younger the students, the more practical it is for the teacher to preselect Web sites for this project or any other. As they get older, encourage them to find what they need so they can have a chance to evaluate and understand the differences between quality references. Here is a suggested Web site for use with this project: National Geographic Photographs http://www.nationalgeographic.com/photography/.

National Geographic is known worldwide for its photographs of people, places, and events. National Geographic's photographers have captured both historical and newsworthy events. On this site, students can view the photos and read the captions and other stories related to the taking of the picture.

Process

- Go through the newspaper with students looking at the photographs and the captions.
- Ask the students if they think the caption and the photograph match.
- Allow students to look through the rest of the newspaper for five minutes, looking for other photographs.
- Ask students whether they can tell what is going on in the picture without the caption. What does the caption help them to understand?
- Divide the students into groups of two to four.
- Access (via the National Geographic Web site or other preselected Web sites) and locate photographs of different events. Allow students to print four or five photographs.

Make sure that the captions for each photograph are included with the photograph.

- Allow the students to discuss the photographs as pieces of art, either in small groups or as a class. Talk about impact, beauty, and other artistic qualities.

- Allow the students to discuss the photographs as stories, either in small groups or as a class. Talk about themes, subjects, and narratives.

- Encourage the students to work through each photograph and caption. They should read the caption and then look at the photograph to understand how the photograph conveys the caption. They should identify the elements in the photograph (places, people, and things) that the caption describes.

- Encourage students to look through the series of photographs and put the story together.

PART 2: WRITING CAPTIONS

Materials

- Student photographs of an event. Encourage students to bring in three or four of their own photographs from a single event or day.

- If possible and time permitting, allow the group to take three or four photographs of themselves during an event.

Process

- Look at each of their photographs and list the elements— place, people, actions, and so on. This can be done individually or as a group.

- Have students write one-to-two-sentence captions for each photograph in the series. Encourage the students to write the captions across as a series so that it will eventually become a photographic essay.

- Ask the students to exchange their photo essay with another group of students. That group of students should be able to explain the events by reading the captions and the photographs.

- Identify and resolve any problems with the photo essays based on comments from the other group.

Assessment

Students can be assessed based on participation, quality of captions (grammar and content), and insight.

Reflection

Writing captions is one of the most enjoyable activities to give students of any age group. A very basic and fun way to start with this activity would be to create text bubbles, in which the students can imagine what they think the individuals in the photograph are saying. Students can do this with advertisements and with other forms of visual text.

Transitioning to captions will then be easy. Ask them now to document what is actually happening. Each of these activities provides a connection to the multiple forms of literacy.

LESSON 7.3: CROP CRAZY

Before You Begin

Familiarize yourself with certain photographic terms such as *crop* and *airbrushing*. Discuss with students if they have ever changed their pictures for any reason. Have they cropped a picture? Have they eliminated red eye?

Objectives

1. Students will learn the photographic term *cropping*.
2. Students will use a framing tool to understand how you can eliminate or add details to a photo through this method.

Materials

- Magazine covers, newspaper photos, and any other photos you wish to use. Here is a list of suggested places for locating photographs for this exercise:
  - *Discovery Girls*
  - *Girls Life*

- *Kids Discover*
- *Muse*
- *National Geographic for Kids*
- *Newsweek*
- *People* or *Teen People*
- *Sports Illustrated* or *Sports Illustrated for Kids*
- *Time*

- A cropping tool that has been placed on top of twenty-five photographs. See Supplement 7B.

Process

- Define with students words such as *crop*, *frame*, and so on prior to beginning the lesson.
- Break students up into groups of two to four and distribute precropped photos.
- Analyze by using a framing tool how little or how much a photograph can tell depending on how an image is cropped.
- Ask students to uncrop their photos and talk about what they are seeing as they uncover.
- Go to each table and sit in, assisting students in answering the following questions:

  - What is the message when a photo is cropped?
  - Is it positive or is it negative?
  - What makes the image important?
  - Why would a photographer or editor choose to crop or eliminate information from a particular photo?
  - Is that ethical if it is a news photograph?

- Discuss with students how each person has a unique perspective and may not see things similarly. As you work your way around the classroom students will have a variety of thoughts on the stories they see reflected in the images.

Assessment

Students will be evaluated through observations of their collaborative efforts in coming up with responses. Teacher assessment will also take place through informal conferencing while joining the working groups, listening to students' conversation, and observing their responses.

Reflection

Cropping is a fun activity for students. It also provides immediate enlightenment. As students learn about the concept, they are able to perform it and therefore able to recognize right away how cropping can be useful or dangerous depending on the message that the photo creates.

LESSON 7.4: PHOTO MANIPULATION

Before You Begin

This continues the ideas presented in the previous lesson, by demonstrating to students how easy it is to change the idea of a photo with just a few quick changes. Photo manipulation exists in a multitude of ways, but it is clearly seen in magazines where models are shown on the front covers. Magazines such as *YM* and *Teen People*, or for older students *Seventeen, Vogue*, and *GQ*, show how easily magazines can show pictures of models with no blemishes, wrinkles, or lines. This introduces the idea of what is real versus what is not real. In a recent article, actress Kate Winslet, best known for her role in *Titanic*, bemoaned the fact that she was airbrushed for the cover of *GQ* magazine; her body was replaced with the body of a model. "I do not look like that and more importantly I don't desire to look like that. I am proud, you know. It's hard work getting your shape back after two kids but I like the way I look," Winslet stated after the *GQ* airbrushing incident.

Newspapers and news magazines have also changed photographs to meet the editorial needs of a story. One of the most famous examples of photo manipulation is the O. J. Simpson picture on the cover of *Time* and *Newsweek* from June 27, 1994. More recently, a *Los Angeles Times* staff photographer combined two of his Iraqi photographs into one to "improve" the composition, thereby changing the context of the message. Discussions of ethics, truth, and bias need to take place in order to extend knowledge on how and why these photographs are the equivalent of direct quotations.

Objectives

1. Students will be able to understand the concept of photo manipulation, altering images so that they misrepresent the information presented or in some cases telling a lie through a camera.
2. Students will be able to analyze a photograph and detect where information has been manipulated and changed.

Materials

- A selection of front covers from newsmagazines such as *Time* and *Newsweek*.
- The June 27, 1994 covers of *Newsweek* and *Time* depicting the two variations of the O. J. Simpson mug shot.
- The ethical statement of news photographers from the National Press Photographers Association: http://www .nppa.org/.
- A good selection of photographs from magazines or newspapers, enough for the whole class.

Process

- Define photo manipulation for students.
- Introduce the magazine covers and briefly talk about what the photos say about what is going on in each issue.
- Ask students if they think this is an original photo or if something has been changed. There will be a wide range of feelings about this question.
- Introduce the *Time* and *Newsweek* photo of O. J. Simpson and any photos that you may have found that have been digitally changed for news presentation.
- Ask students:
  - What is the difference?
  - Which do you think is the real photo?
  - Why would someone choose to darken the picture of a person?
  - What is the message to you, the reader?
  - Introduce the concept of ethics: What does it mean, and should photographers have an ethical standard to follow?
- Ask students what they think of photo manipulation. There will be both points of view. Ask students to explain their philosophical beliefs on this issue.
- Introduce the concepts of ethics and its meaning:
  - Ethics—a set of moral principles or values; the principles of conduct governing an individual or a group.
- Bring the conversation to news and the importance of news photos.
  - Should news photos be changed or cropped?

- Review some of the issues with cropping too much from a photograph. Students understand the idea of eliminating a bad shot or an angle from a shot, but when you start to talk to them about important items like war or the World Trade Center their feelings begin to change.

Assessment

Students can be assessed based on participation, quality of responses, and how they interact with each other.

Reflection

The concepts of photo manipulation and ethics elicit very strong opinions. Photo manipulation of models introduces the discussion of body image. Photos influence women's ideas of what people look like. Boys will also have contributions on this topic, unique to their own difficulties with body image. This lesson can be changed and manipulated in order to incorporate whatever topics come up in the classroom.

LESSON 7.5: PULITZER PRIZE PHOTOS

Before You Begin

This activity is set up in the style of a classroom museum, also known as the "classeum." The artifacts are the pictures, and the students' role is to observe the images presented and analyze what they are seeing. The photos are amazing and they will both horrify and enlighten your students. Therefore, it is very important that you are careful with the selection of images. Students should not see the photos until the actual day of the lesson.

Should you have a classroom that does not lend itself to the museum setup, consider going to the computer lab and visiting the Pulitzer Prize Web site. This site will allow you to do the same activity online.

Objective

Students will understand the importance of Pulitzer Prize photos as compared to manipulated photos.

Materials

- Book: *Capture the Moment: The Pulitzer Prize Photos* edited by Cyma Rubin and Eric Newton, two copies.
- Pulitzer Prize photos matted on 11 × 17 hard bond paper and hung throughout the classroom.
    - It will take approximately two days to prepare for the class museum. You will need two copies of *Capture the Moment: The Pulitzer Prize Photos*, because photos are printed back to back and you may want to use two photos that cannot be separated. Tear out the photos you have selected. The actual pictures span the size of an 11 × 17 sheet of paper. You should obtain some card stock paper that is larger than this size and either glue or rubber cement the photos down. Wait a day in order for the glue or rubber cement to set, and then laminate the posters so that they do not fall apart and can withstand disturbance throughout the activity.
- Student reflective worksheet for analysis. See Supplement 7C.

Web Site

The Pulitzer Prize: www.pulitzer.org
The Pulitzer Prize Web site features an archive of winners. Full text and photographs for journalism prizes are featured for years 1995–2005 only. To access the photographs, select a year (1995–2005), select either "Spot News Photography" or "Feature Photography" Prizes, and then select the "Works" tab.

Process

- Set up the classroom in a museum format so the students will feel free to walk around, sit or stand, gaze at the photos, and read the photographers' stories uninterrupted.
- As the students settle into their seats, hand out the analysis sheet Capturing the Prize: A Photo Analysis (Supplement 7C).
- Explain to students that there are a number of photographs around the room. The photographs show times of triumph, sadness, and some of the darkest moments in our history. They were photographs captured on film by photographers who were willing to go the extra mile in

order to show the world, through their lens, these images. Their job is to walk around the room and look carefully at the photos. Have them read the stories associated with the photographers who snapped the pictures.

- Ask students to select two photos and write about them. They are to answer the questions:

  - What made you stop and look at the photograph?
  - What made you decide to write about this photograph?
  - What was it that struck you?
  - How did the photograph make you feel?
  - They are to write as much as possible, but a minimum of two paragraphs.

- Remind students that photographs are a personal experience. They are not to pick a photo just because their fellow classmate and friend did. (This needs to be emphasized in seventh and eighth grade, but not usually in the older grades.) Instead tell students to pick photos that made them think or were heartfelt.

- Assist students with the discussion of photographs as you walk around observing what pictures grab their attention. In some cases, give further direction, but for the most part you can watch students as they react to the images and the stories presented before them.

- Leave ten minutes at the end of class for students to share their thoughts on the photos.

- Close the class with a reminder of the true purpose of photographs and why Pulitzer Prize photos have impacted our society for generations.

Assessment

Students will be assessed on how well they work through the photographs and their final reflections.

Reflection

This class becomes a very quiet and calming experience for both the teacher and students. The pictures themselves are overwhelming, which quiets everything else that goes on in the classroom. It is important to maintain this kind of silence as much as possible, for it enhances the students' perceptions and learning that goes on throughout this activity. You will come away amazed by the depth of their responses.

SUPPLEMENT 7A: PHOTOGRAPHIC TERMS

- **Airbrushing:** Method of retouching black and white or color photographs by spraying dye under pressure onto selected areas of the negative or print.

- **Camera angles:** Various positions of the camera with respect to the subject being photographed, each giving a different viewpoint and perspective.

- **Composition:** Visual arrangement of all the elements in a photograph.

- **Cropping:** Omitting parts of an image when making a print or copy negative in order to improve or change the composition of the final image.

- **Ethics:** A set of moral principles or values; the principles of conduct governing an individual or a group.

- **Photo aesthetics:** An artistically beautiful or pleasing image, usually composed by a variety of factors including lighting, exposure, and angles.

- **Photo manipulation:** Altering images so that they misrepresent the information or in some cases telling a lie through a camera.

SUPPLEMENT 7B: CROPPING TOOL

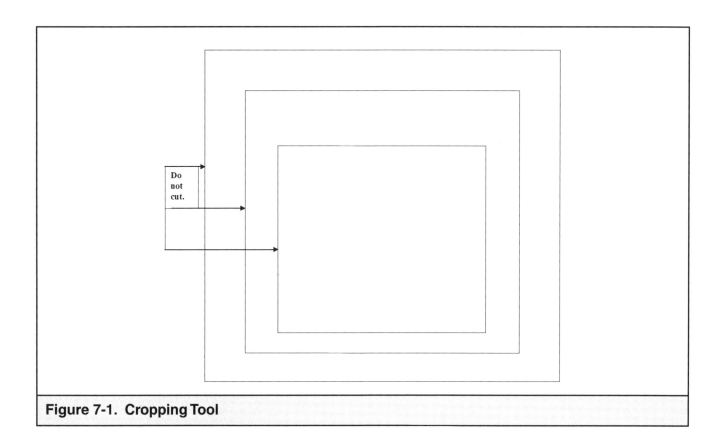

Figure 7-1. Cropping Tool

Directions:

1. Do not cut the left side of boxes.
2. Only cut the right side of the two inner boxes, as if doing an inverted C.
3. Place this cutout on top of the selected photograph.
4. Proceed accordingly.

SUPPLEMENT 7C: CAPTURING THE PRIZE: A PHOTO ANALYSIS

Welcome to the "Photo Classeum"! There are a number of photographs around the room. Some of them are extremely troubling and some will make you smile. They are moments in time captured on film by photographers who were willing to go the extra mile.

Your job is to walk around the room and look carefully at the photos. Read the stories associated with the photographer who snapped the pictures. Select two photos and write about them. Write a brief analysis of their impact on you. Why did you pick the photograph? What was it that struck you? How did the photograph make you feel? You need to write a minimum of two complete paragraphs for each photograph, but feel free to keep writing and use the back of this sheet to continue your thought process.

Keep in mind that photographs are a personal experience. They make you feel something about the image. Not everyone will pick the same picture. Just pick the ones that captured your attention or your heart.

PHOTOGRAPH 1

TITLE _____

_____
_____
_____
_____
_____
_____
_____
_____
_____
_____
_____
_____
_____
_____
_____
_____
_____
_____
_____
_____
_____

PHOTOGRAPH 2

TITLE _____

_____

_____

_____

_____

_____

_____

_____

_____

_____

_____

_____

_____

_____

_____

_____

_____

_____

_____

_____

REFERENCES

Newseum. 1997. *Is Seeing Believing?* Washington, DC: Newseum.
Rubin, Cyma, and Eric Newton. 2001. *Capture the Moment: The Pulitzer Prize Photos*. New York: W. W. Norton.

MUSIC AND RADIO

"Much of the pleasure of popular music for young people lies in the sense that it 'belongs' to its listeners, that it is precisely 'theirs' and not 'ours.'"

—David Buckingham, Hardcore Rappin':
Popular Music, Identity and Critical Discourse

CHAPTER OVERVIEW

The bobbing of students' heads to the rhythm of music is a commonplace occurrence. With new technologies such as iPods and V-Cast technology in cell phones, it is without question that music captivates and motivates this generation.

Music's influence has never been broader. There are many lessons to be learned by studying mainstream artists in rock, rap, hip-hop, country, soul, and pop. Music often tells a story or communicates an emotion. We all can recall songs that remind us of special events, birthdays, marriages, and even breakups. The same is true for today's youth. Music is a sign of independence because it creates feelings of power and energy that, once felt, are hard to escape. The music of today's teenagers is more raw, reaching depths that are unexpected to parents and teachers. This is due, to a certain degree, to the artists, who have become rawer as well. Raw, in this context, means graphic, and it can be a way for students to connect with themselves and their own growing pains.

The themes of music are in many ways unchanging: love (from falling in love to the loss of love), heartache, relationships, anger, and rebellion. However, there have been some subtle and definitive changes between the music of the 1960s and 1970s and music since 2000. Bob Dylan vocalized Vietnam and discussions on drugs, death, and dying. Today we have music that talks about abuse, rape, hate, a little bit about the Gulf War, and more about sex in its most graphic form, including clothing such as the "thong" that sexualized a generation. At the time of this writing, some of the most popular songs receiving airplay are *Promiscuous* by Nelly Furtado, *Unfaithful* by Rihanna, *My Hump* by Black Eyed Peas, and *Shake That* by Eminem. Some of the titles give you a good idea of what the topic of the song is and how graphic some of the lyrics have become. We hear students as young as ten years old singing these songs because they have a rhythm and beat that are appealing. Even adults have a hard time separating the lyrics from the beat. How are we to expect our students to be capable of this without any kind of instruction? While we don't always want to, we must help to make them aware of the messages sent out to the mainstream.

Figure 8-1. "Music" by Lynn Johnston
(**FOR BETTER OR FOR WORSE** © 2003 Lynn Johnston Productions. Dist. By Universal Press Syndicate. Reprinted with permission. All rights reserved.)

The other main difference between music of the past and the music of the future is what MTV has done to change how music is communicated to audiences. MTV began in 1980 and changed the way people looked and listened to music. MTV is currently celebrating its twenty-fifth anniversary. The following are some notable facts about MTV, presented by the Associated Press on July 31, 2006. These facts could be considered for possible future lessons.

- The Debut: August 1, 1981. The first video? The slyly prophetic "Video Killed the Radio Star" by the now-forgotten Buggles. Only a few thousand people on a single cable system in northern New Jersey could see it. Sometimes the screen would go black when someone at MTV inserted a tape into a VCR. Within a few years, millions of kids demanded that their parents buy cable so they could see MTV.

- Beat It: March 31, 1983. Michael Jackson became the first black artist with a video on MTV. The segregation was MTV's early shame, which is ironic, considering its later role in popularizing rap. And the early snub wasn't forgotten: "You don't have all of music television when you are leaving things out," says Los Lonely Boys singer Henry Garza.

- Madonna Busts Out: September 14, 1984. Performing "Like a Virgin" at the first Video Music Awards, Madonna popped out of a cake dressed in a wedding gown and writhed through her hit. At that moment, Madonna became a superstar, put the Video Music Awards on the map, and set an enduring tone.

- Money for Nothing: 1985. The Dire Straits song was about MTV, mocked MTV, and became the band's biggest hit because of MTV. It was one of the first videos to feature computer animation, and Sting made a clever cameo echoing his role in iconic "I want my MTV" ads. The rules for music stardom had changed.

- Rap Blasts Off: August 6, 1986. It's no coincidence that "Yo! MTV Raps!" premiered about the same time rap started becoming the dominant music form for young America. Hip white kids like Rick Rubin or the Beastie Boys may have loved rap before, but "Yo! MTV Raps!" brought it into every suburban living room.

- Enter Grunge: September 29, 1991. Nirvana's "Smells Like Teen Spirit" video killed the hair metal scene and signaled the ascendancy of grunge. The images themselves were arresting, with tattooed cheerleaders and what seemed like an underwater pep rally in a dank gymnasium.

- $#*!: March 5, 2002. Sharrrr-rronnnn! The first bleeped-out swear word on The Osbournes' premiere was followed by fifty-eight others. For a while, the foggy-headed rocker, his type-A wife, and his self-involved kids became America's first family, if only for the sheer weirdness of their life (Bauder, 2006).

The following lessons are not intended to negate the importance of music in our students' lives. The role of the classroom teacher or school library media specialist is not to tell a student that their music is bad or that music is unimportant. It isn't true; the truth is, some of us like the same music as our students! Beyond that point, music serves a vital role in our society and is influential to all of us whether we are young or old. Music touches our lives so much that globally we spend $40 billion annually, as estimated by the Recording Industry Association of America. The U.S. recording industry accounts for fully one-third of that world market. This is an astronomical figure considering that 20 percent is spent by today's youth. They are the target market for the entertainment industry, and there is a billion-dollar price tag attached.

This chapter asks you to turn the tables by considering the teachable lessons and moments in popular music. These lessons help students understand the choices they make about their music and how it affects their lives, from the clothes that they wear and the things that they say to how they think. The goal of this project is to give students an opportunity to study how the industry determines what they are hearing. Some of the topics covered include censorship, stereotypes, and body image.

Grade Level: Although these lessons have been primarily used in a classroom environment for grades five through eight, they are adaptable to all grade levels. You determine what best fits your classroom.

Curriculum Connections:	1. English—Reading, writing, and composition.
	2. Social Studies—Historical significance of sound and terminology.
	3. Arts—This unit fits well into the applied arts curriculum.
Media Literacy Connections:	1. All media messages are constructed.
	2. Media messages are constructed using a creative language with its own rules.
	3. Different people experience the same media message differently.
	4. Media are primarily businesses driven by a profit motive.
	5. Media have embedded values and points of view.
Time Frame:	These lessons can be used in a fifty-minute period. Keep in mind that the activity may continue beyond this time period, depending on the level of participation.

LESSON 8.1: MUSIC GENRES

Before You Begin

This is the introductory lesson to music genres and vocabulary associated with the music industry. Through listening to a variety of music, students will become familiar with several genres of music. They will learn how music receives airplay and how popularity is determined. The goal is for each student to appreciate that there are diverse listeners and that music produced all over the world provides pleasure for different listening populations.

Objectives

1. Students will understand how and why different people experience the same media message differently.
2. Students will evaluate the kinds of popular music.
3. Students will comprehend why music is so important to many people.

Materials

- The only equipment needed for this lesson is a CD player or a computer with speakers. You can also use music sites such as Yahoo's Launchcast, http://launch.yahoo.com/launchcast/stations/, which plays songs or videos.

- Bring to class a random sampling of ten CDs representative of the type of music that students listen to. Music selected should cover a wide variety of genres such as hip-hop, country, and rap. Many artists have been mainstream for a number of years, while others recently became popular. You should preview all lyrics before presenting songs in the classroom, as they can be problematic for discussion because they may be too inappropriate for the school to feel comfortable with, as related to administrators and parents. Several artists release "clean versions" which convey the same messages as the originals but without some of the questionable language. Whichever you and your administrators are more comfortable using is what you should present within the context of your classroom.

- Note: As the school library media specialist or classroom teacher, you can ask the students to bring in CDs. Many students have iPod speakers. One could bring them in and students could play tunes off their iPods.

Process

- Begin the class by asking the meaning of the term *genre*.
  - List several different types of music:
    - Pop
    - Rap
    - Country
    - Hip-hop
    - Opera
    - Musicals
- This may also be an opportune time to introduce other music vocabulary. (See Supplement 8A.)
- Pick ten CDs representative of the type of music students listen to regularly. The goal here is to make sure that the music is mainstream to teen culture.
- Ask the class:
  - Why is music so important to us?
  - Why do we like the music we do?

- Play a series of songs from the different CDs. Have students write what they liked or disliked about each piece of music.

Assessment

Students can be assigned a journal entry from Supplement 8B to use as a reflection exercise to assess their knowledge of the content presented. Students can also be assessed on participation and quality of insights.

Reflection

As mentioned in the introduction to this lesson, music is a personal experience for teens, especially because they relate it to their lives and their activities. Middle school students will especially gravitate to music that is controversial and violent. This lesson opens up the doorway to conversations that can change their perspective on music. Understanding that music genres are diverse and that each person has a distinct reason for what he or she listens to allows healthy guided discussions to take place.

While some adults would consider running away from this lesson, it has been very beneficial in my experience. Students want to share their favorite songs with you and their peers. They also want you to help them vocalize their love of a certain type of music. As with many other media projects, this may require some restraint on your part so that you don't blurt out how much you detest an artist or certain controversial messages. Teachers should remain as neutral as possible while facilitating the discussion. Use this lesson as an opportunity to listen to what students have to say about the messages they receive from musical artists. It may provide you with many ideas for future lessons.

Future Exercise

Once you become comfortable with this topic, you may want to consider allowing students to pick a favorite CD and bring it to class as a show-and-tell piece. You must be aware that the music they bring in may not be what you would consider appropriate, and it is important to have this discussion with students. You should also tell students that you will only play selections of music and that those selections must be G-rated.

LESSON 8.2: THE MUSIC VIDEO

Before You Begin

Many videos are appropriate for school and can be viewed without any concerns. There are just as many that will cause you great stress if you are not aware of the content.

**ALWAYS PREVIEW A VIDEO BEFORE SHOWING IT
TO THE CLASS!**

Yes, this is in capital letters and bold because as with any other subject, you do not want to be surprised or embarrassed by images appearing on your screen. A friend of mine who taught third grade told me of an embarrassing incident where she was showing a movie on dolphins and, in her rush, did not think that there would be any problems with showing information about such an innocent animal. However, she did not realize what the actual mating practice was for a dolphin and that it was included in the video. To her horror, the whole event was shown in great detail on tape and she had to quickly turn it off and come up with a plausible explanation. While this example is unrelated to music, it shows how easy it is to let something slip by. While you may be able to cover up some items in front of third graders, middle and high schoolers will not let you get away so easily.

Objectives

1. Students will understand media messages are constructed using a creative language with its own rules.
2. Students will discuss some of the controversial topics raised by music, such as love, sex, drugs, and violence.
3. Students will explore popular culture and how trends correlate with music.

Materials

- A TV and VCR or DVD player.
- You may want to consider getting a membership to Yahoo Launchcast, which streams music videos constantly. This will require a high speed connection to the Internet or a T1 line in your school building. The service is free when you sign up for an email account with Yahoo.
- A segment of the PBS broadcast of *In the Mix: Media Literacy: TV—What You Don't See!* This VHS/DVD can

be used with other media literacy lessons, but there is a segment devoted specifically to music videos. The segments are brief, which works very well for forty- to fifty-minute class periods. This particular segment is four minutes long.

- Summary: Teens take a close-up look at the images and messages portrayed in hip-hop music videos. We hear from record company executives and popular artists, MC Lyte and The Roots, about how the images of barely dressed women, fancy cars, and unlimited alcohol are used in music videos to sell albums. Following their brief interview, The Roots discuss the production of a video called *What They Do*, which deconstructs these video images using humorous subtitles.

- Consider also using VH-1 segments of *Pop-Up Video* or *Behind the Scenes*, which provides an analysis of what takes place during the production of a video and also includes notes on the musical artists.

Process

- Set up the classroom for a viewing and discussion piece. Be sure that each student is able to hear and listen to the words of the video and the commentary by the various musical artists. Providing lyric sheets for students may be worthwhile because the lyrics are not always audible.
- Ask students:

  - Do they sit and watch videos regularly?
  - What makes a video attractive?
  - Do they have a favorite music video and if so, what is it?

- Introduce the media literacy concept: media messages are constructed using a creative language with its own rules, and discuss what that means for music videos.

  - Creative language is not just words but also the unspoken meaning.

- Introduce a music video of your choice.

  - Students will watch the video without any sound and make notes of the images they are seeing, the colors, and what they think is happening.
    - They should note the following:

- The relationship they are seeing between men and women
- The gender and race of the video participants
- Violence, if any
- How women are portrayed

- Students will watch the video with sound and follow up on their previous notes.
  - They should also consider how the lyrics make them feel. Do these images affect their attitudes and behaviors? Hearing a song versus seeing a song displayed on video can change perceptions either from positive to negative or the opposite.

- Show the segment of the PBS broadcast of *In the Mix: Media Literacy: TV—What You Don't See!*

  - Discuss the following points with students:
    - What are typical images shown in hip-hop music videos?
    - How do relationships play out in a music video?
    - Were they surprised by what they learned in The Roots' mock video?

Assessment

Collect class notes that were taken throughout the viewing of the music videos. These can be used as a part of your assessment along with participation and quality of insights. Once again, you may want to consider selecting a journal entry topic from Supplement 8B.

Reflection

This is truly one of the most enjoyable lessons to cover with students. Visual and musical aids that accompany any lesson are sure to attract attention. This lesson comes right from their own teenage backyards. Students like to point out what they are able to see throughout the video, and they like to see it played over and over again. However, they aren't used to turning off the sound and just watching a video. It is usually a new experience for them, but it helps them to focus on the messages that are represented in the music.

LESSON 8.3: THE MUSIC INDUSTRY

Before You Begin

While students believe that there are dozens or even hundreds of influential record companies, this is simply not the case. Big-name companies such as Virgin are owned by even bigger companies such as EMI. This lesson helps students understand who owns what company and why it seems like much of the music out there is the same. Part of this lesson will take them into the work of big media conglomerates in order to see how they have shrunk the capabilities of the music industry so that only four companies produce, manufacture, distribute, and promote much of the world's media.

Objectives

1. Students will see that media companies are primarily businesses driven by a profit motive.
2. Students will find out who represents the music industry.
3. Students will examine why the music industry picks the artists they do to popularize.
4. Students will investigate music labels and see if their choices are limited.

Materials

- Provide students with a list of conglomerates and record labels:

  - EMI, which includes Virgin/Atlantic, Angel, Blue Note, Capitol, European Columbia, Elektrola, Odeon, Parlophone, Pathé Marconi, Positiva, and others
  - Sony BMG Music Entertainment, which includes Arista, (American) Columbia, Epic, J, Jive, LaFace, Ravenous, RCA, and others
  - Universal Music Group, which includes A&M, Decca/London, Deutsche Grammophon, Geffen, Interscope, Island Def Jam, Motown, Philips, Rampagge, Universal, and others
  - Warner Music Group, which includes Asylum, Atlantic, Elektra, Erato, Heiress, Reprise, Rhino, Rykodisc, Sire, Sub, and others

- You will need a computer lab for students to research and make the connections to music labels and media ownership.

Process

- Define *music label* and *music conglomerates*.
- Provide a list of the labels for students, but do not include the conglomerates.
- Discuss the media literacy concept: media are primarily businesses driven by a profit motive.
- Ask students:

  - What does the word *profit* mean?
    - You can use a variety of examples in order to demonstrate the concept of profit. Include an example as basic as buying groceries. In previous classes, we have taken clothing and deconstructed the cost of developing a GAP shirt or a Nike sneaker. Big-name products are the best to use because there is such a huge price markup.

  - Who do they think makes money in the music industry?
    - Most students think that the singer of the song is who makes all the money. They don't realize that music artists make the bulk of their money from concerts, which is why many musicians leave their label and produce independently once they have made enough money.

- Take the list of record labels and pair students up to research who owns each label. This has a scavenger hunt feel to it. This may take more than one period depending on how proficient your students are in the use of search engines.

  - Students can list their responses independently, or you could have them put their answers on a large sheet of butcher paper. Since there are only four conglomerates, this is possible to do without compromising too much of the classroom. Another option is to use Inspiration Software and have students develop a flowchart that delineates ownership.

- Close class with a discussion of their findings. Were there any surprises in their search?

- Note: In a future class, you may want to make this listing bigger by having students choose their favorite music artist, find which label carries their music, and then find who owns the label.

Assessment

The students' graphs, lists, or spreadsheets will be your assessment of how they were able to understand the information presented in this lesson. Since students will be working in pairs or groups, you may also want to supply a participation grade that covers collaboration, work ethic, and effort. If you are involved in any kind of technology assessment, you may also want to use how they use a particular program such as Inspiration to produce their work.

Reflection

This lesson gives students the big picture behind why breaking into the music industry can be very difficult. It also helps them to understand basic business concepts of profit and gain. Students will be able to see how music companies limit the choices offered to the general public. When students see that music is owned by only a few companies, they are generally surprised. While doing this lesson they also see that other products and media are owned by the same people who own the record label. Students will learn where their money is going when they buy into the media messages provided by the music industry.

LESSON 8.4: MUSIC AND CENSORSHIP

Before You Begin

Teachers and school library media specialists have certainly heard plenty about censorship, especially in relation to books. You probably have had red flags go up about some literature selections. Rarely, though, do we discuss the censorship of music. In the last few years, there has been an obvious cleaning up of certain lyrics due to their controversial themes. However, censorship exists in other ways. We no longer hear about some artists because of their political actions or because people believe their messages are no longer important. This lesson provides you with ways to demonstrate how censorship has come to play a role in the music industry.

Objectives

1. Students will become familiar with the media literacy concept that all media messages are constructed.
2. Students will understand how censorship works in the music industry.

Materials

- For this lesson, you will need to have both a CD player and DVD player or a way to transmit music videos.
- Yahoo Launchcast or another media program can be used to stream music videos.
- You will need to find a song and a video which are currently being dropped from airplay. You will be able to find such items by reviewing *Billboard* and other current radio play magazines. Controversial music has become an issue with the involvement of the FCC (Federal Communications Commission) as well as the current political framework.
    - At the time of this writing, one group not receiving as much radio play as it used to because of political actions is the Dixie Chicks.
    - You can certainly find controversial artists especially in the hip-hop genre. Once again, it is important to select items that you are comfortable discussing with students.
- Note: You might instead wish to discuss radio disc jockeys. High school students could discuss Howard Stern.

Process

- Discuss the media literacy concept: all media messages are constructed.
- Introduce the term *censorship*. Define censorship of books and then censorship of music.
- Have students list musical artists who are considered controversial. Here are a few examples:
    - Dixie Chicks—Country
    - Eminem—Rap
    - Black Eyed Peas—Hip-hop
- Have students list what they think these artists have in common.

- Distribute to the class the lyrics of songs that have been changed for airplay. One of the tamest ones to use is by the music group Black Eyed Peas: *Let's Get This Party Started*, which is heard on the radio differently from the way it was originally written.

- Have students listen to the song heard on the radio and then compare it with the one recorded on the CD.

- Ask students:

    - Why are lyrics changed?

    - How does it affect the song and the artist?

    - What impact does it have on the listener?

    - Is censorship acceptable at times, or should it be prevented?

        - The answers to this question will provide you with insights on what students think is acceptable, what their parents say is acceptable, and what society says is acceptable.

- Find a controversial music video and repeat the same process.

Assessment

Collect students' class notes from this lesson. These can be used as a part of your assessment along with participation and quality of insights. Once again, you may want to consider selecting a journal entry topic from Supplement 8B. Students have strong feelings on the subject of censorship which they want to share, and they can more freely do so on paper.

Reflection

As mentioned previously, this can be a tricky lesson if you have not previewed the song lyrics or the video. You may want to have the music teacher help you find music that would work for this class or take suggestions from classroom teachers.

LESSON 8.5: MUSIC: CULTURE AND IMAGE

Before You Begin

The music industry prides itself on encouraging fads, looks, and styles. The musical artist comes with a full package of promotional materials which later generate more profits for these businesses. When Britney Spears came onto the scene, she boosted the sales of midriff shirts and thongs. Rap artists have promoted the wearing of jeans far below the waist or hips. Flashy jewelry called "bling" is another source of business.

At the same time, the industry has promoted certain images of men and women. Men are seen as either tender heartthrobs or brutal, violent contenders. Women are shown as thin, extremely thin in some cases, showing off so much as to leave nothing to the imagination. Then there are the sneakers, pumps, and stilettos that have grown more and more popular. All of these items make up the culture and image in music.

Objectives

1. Students will learn that media have embedded values and points of view.
2. Students will learn what marketing tools are used to encourage their buying power in the direction of music.

Materials

- There are two videos or DVDs that you will need for this lesson.

  - The first you will need to collect beforehand from stations such as MTV, BET, or VH1. You only need twenty to thirty seconds of each video to show different pop styles. This tape will need to be updated each year as music and styles change.

  - The second video is from PBS and is called *Merchants of Cool*. This video deals specifically with the idea of "cool" and how conglomerates such as MTV represent images to youth. The producer of this video looks at the images of men and women and discusses this impact on teens. The focus is on the music industry and its impact on this generation of children. While this video is becoming dated, the content is quite pertinent.

- Later in the tape, there are some graphic pieces that you may not want to show in class. Select a few clips to share and discuss with students.

• You will also need to have access to a computer lab for research, and you may want to have some music industry magazines such as *Entertainment Weekly* or *Rolling Stone* available for students to use.

Process

• Discuss media literacy concept: media have embedded values and points of view.

• Ask students:

- How does pop culture tie in with the music industry?

- What kinds of items, other than clothing, are marketed as part of the music scene?

- What does the clothing say about the musician and you?

• First, show students the clips you preselected. This should take no more than five to ten minutes.

- Students should take notes with this central question in mind:

- What types of clothing or brands did they notice these pop icons wearing?

- Once the video is complete, have students share what they just viewed. Make sure that you select and listen equally to both the girl students and the boy students. Both sexes are usually very surprised at the comments.

• Next, show a small segment of *Merchants of Cool*. Once again, you don't want to go past five to ten minutes.

• Ask students:

- What does "cool" mean?

- Are they surprised at how the music industry is tracking them in order to capture that idea of "cool"?

• Have students pick a music celebrity and write a profile of all the goods they market to youth. The teacher should provide a list of suggestions. This should be at least one page long. Students should be able to answer the following questions about their artist:

- What makes the person you chose popular?
- What kinds of ads have you seen which pictured a musician?
- What techniques are used to convey the messages?
- Name some of the selected goods marketed by this artist. What can you buy that would be representative of them? For example, both Jessica Simpson and Jennifer Lopez have their own perfumes.
- What would make you consider purchasing any of these items?
- Is it worth purchasing products that are marketed by celebrities?
- What have you learned from this lesson about the image and culture of the music industry?

Assessment

Student assessment should be based on the report they produce on their musical artist. You can decide how long you would like the report, and certainly restructure the questions to fit your classroom situation. Once again, you can use student participation and quality of insights as a part of their evaluation.

Reflection

"Cool" is a very important part of teenage life. While some will admit that this is what they strive for, some will deny this claim. Most will say that they struggle with their self-image because of media messages, especially ones reflected through the music industry. These messages have been something they contend with either personally or via their peers. Be aware that this lesson may open conversations into other areas related to students' health such as anorexia and bulimia.

SUPPLEMENT 8A: MUSIC TERMINOLOGY

Alternative music: A term that came to be used in the 1980s to describe music that was not a part of the mainstream genres; in most cases it described punk rock. In the 1990s this term began referring to grunge bands.

Hip-hop: A form of urban, African American music that became popular during the 1970s; its current association is with dancing as much as a genre of music. Some people claim it is synonymous with rap.

Lyrics: The words of a song.

Popular music: The music frequently played on radio stations targeting the teen population; considered a version of rock 'n' roll with lyrics that have more to do with romantic love.

Rap: A style of music with components consisting of rhythmic lyrics that are spoken over the backdrop of music beat, scratching, and mixing; formerly known as MCing with an accompaniment of DJing.

Record label: A name brand of a company that specializes in the manufacturing, distributing, and promotion of audio and video recordings; examples of record labels are Virgin/Atlantic and Sony BMG Music Entertainment.

Rock 'n' roll: A form of popular music that includes a band consisting of electric guitars, drums, and/or various other instruments. This genre has had a cultural impact on society more than any other form of music.

Trend: A current style or preference.

SUPPLEMENT 8B: JOURNALS

Journaling encourages students' ability to discern information while also providing student and teacher with an assessment of the growth of knowledge in the study of media literacy. Teachers can provide writing prompts for the student or allow the students to create their own topic. Music media literacy lessons are a good time to use a reflection exercise, since their ideas are very personal. This is also a valued way of assessing how students understand the lessons presented and even foreseeing possible questions that may arise in the future. You may consider using some of these topic ideas for future homework assignments:

- Explain your thoughts on the impact music has on people in your age group.
- Pick a CD of your choice. Describe the cover. Write why you like this particular artist's music. List the producer and publisher of the CD.
- Watch MTV, VH1, BET, or CMT and choose a video you would like to write about. Look at the images presented

and describe the messages in the song. Students should note any videos that they find offensive.

- Why are videos so popular? What makes a video attractive to you?
- If you are upset about the images in music videos, what can you do about it?
- Read through a teen magazine such as *Teen*, *Teen People*, or *Seventeen*. Notice the singers and bands that are pictured. Write a list of the types of clothing they wear, the hairstyles, jewelry, shoes, and accessories.
- How does popular culture fit in with hip-hop or other popular music?
- Has your perception of the music industry changed after this week of music study? Why or why not?

SUPPLEMENT 8C: ADDITIONAL ACTIVITIES

INTERVIEW

Students will interview a radio disc jockey via phone, person-to-person, or email to discuss how a song gets radio play. The participating disc jockeys will be listed. Students make the initial call and set up their interview questions. Their report may be given in the form of a newspaper article, not to exceed two pages, although the presentation method can be changed to suit your classroom style.

ACTIVISM/INDUSTRY LETTER

Students will write a letter explaining a concern they have with a video or song that has received airplay via radio or television.

Student Directions: If you are upset about the images in music videos, what can you do? Create a letter to the producer of the video. Be clear about what you find offensive. Make sure that your comments have a global scope as well. Remember to include examples of specific images.

OTHER RESOURCES

Magazines

Billboard—Music charts and genre-specific articles. Very industry oriented. www.billboard.com.

Entertainment Weekly—A guide to staying on top of the media industry. www.ew.com.

Rolling Stone—Contains commentary, reviews on music, and popular culture. Also has articles which demonstrate in-depth reporting on musicians and the industry. www.rollingstone.com.

TV Programs

The following television resources carry industry stories, videos, and other information.

Networks

Black Entertainment Television (BET)—A cable channel which shows hip-hop and R&B music videos as well as religious programming, public affairs programs, and urban-oriented movies and series.

Country Music Television (CMT)—A cable channel focusing on country music, featuring music videos, concerts, movies, and biographies.

Music Television (MTV)—A cable channel that shows youth-oriented music videos, reality shows, and other pop-culture programming.

VH1—A cable channel known for focusing on an older demographic than MTV. Shows music videos, reality shows, and series focusing on pop culture.

Programs

Entertainment Tonight—A daily entertainment news show shown on CBS.

Extra—A syndicated television news program covering entertainment events and celebrities.

WEB SITES

www.adbusters.org—The people who made ad parodies and "culture jamming" famous.

www.mojam.com—Features musician-to-musician resources, news, concert listings, and reviews.

www.musicindustry.com—Offers many support materials for people interested in following issues and opportunities in the industry.

www.riaa.com—Industry-supported group that deals with major issues facing their field, such as censorship.

REFERENCES

Bauder, David. 2006. "From Beavis to Britney: 25 Memorable Moments on MTV's 25th Anniversary." New York: Associated Press, July 31.
Duncan, Barry. 1996. *Mass Media and Popular Culture*. Toronto, Canada: Harcourt-Brace.

ADVERTISING

"We need desperately, I feel, a noncommercial alternative to what commercialism is trying to do to us. I'm not for censorship, but I'm certainly for self-censorship when it comes to producing or purveying products to America's children. I think that for people who make anything for children, their first thought should be: Would I want my child to see, hear or touch this? And if the answer is no, just don't make it."

—("Mister") Fred Rogers

Advertising is perhaps the most important topic covered in this book. Everywhere we go, marketers and advertisers try to attract our attention, and they especially focus on youth. This billion-dollar advertising and marketing machine is devoted to influencing our children's purchasing power, from clothing and food to cars.

Each day thousands of media messages are directed at each of us. The most recent information collected by the Henry J. Kaiser Family Foundation indicated that children view 20,000 television commercials each year. This astronomical figure does not even come close to incorporating the full spectrum of media messages. Ask students where else they encounter advertisements. They will tell you they can be found on buses, billboards, subways, taxis, flyers, church bulletins, and many other places. Ask students if they can think of a place where there is no advertising, and the answer is much more difficult to come by. Even in their homes, and in their most personal space, their bedrooms, advertisements are everywhere. Perhaps the most distinctive way that advertisers have succeeded in marketing and branding teens is through their clothing. Gap, Aeropostale, Abercrombie & Fitch, Old Navy, Hollister, and other clothing lines have become staples in schools across the United States. Marketers' best advertisers have become the children who wear the brand name strewn across their chests and even their bottoms.

Additionally, advertisers have become quite savvy in trying to find ways to fulfill children's needs in products that are normally associated with adults. For example, today's car commercials are not just about the comfort of the adult driver and passenger, but also that of the passenger child who would like his or her own personal cup holder and TV screen for viewing movies. Without question, this method of advertising is quite successful. Children today often participate in the buying process of the adult shopper. Today's youth have a unique power over how their parents spend money.

Advertising also provides many opportunities to teach students how to deconstruct the messages sent to them about the world they live in and the assumptions made about them. The marketing of midriff shirts or tight pants for females and loose jeans for males contributes to the growing sexualization of roles. Advertising messages teach students a distorted version of normalcy by employing extremely thin models and emphasizing certain behaviors by men and women. There are many opportunities for classroom and library media center lessons. The ones provided here are just a small sampling of what can possibly happen in every school.

Besides educating students about the role of the medium of advertising, these lessons will also be the most enjoyable. Why? Because advertisements produced by these marketing companies have become personal and integrated into the lives of the teenage consumer.

Grade Level: These lessons have been primarily used in a classroom environment for grades five through eight, but they are adaptable to all grade levels. You determine what best fits your classroom.

Curriculum Connections:	1. English—Reading, writing, and composition.
	2. Social Studies—Current events.
	3. Math—Marketing and cost analysis.
	4. Science—Ask, find, or determine answers to questions derived from curiosity about everyday experiences. In this particular case, students will study media advertisements.
Media Literacy Connections:	1. All media messages are "constructed."
	2. Media messages are constructed using a creative language.
	3. Media have embedded values, lifestyles and points of view, and omissions.
	4. Most media messages are constructed to gain profit and/or power.
Time Frame:	These lessons can be done within a fifty-minute period, except for one, the Mall Amble. The lesson will require a field trip to a mall in order for students to do some investigation, and it will require a full day. More about this lesson can be found under the lesson plan.

LESSON 9.1: JINGLES, SLOGANS, AND LOGOS

Before You Begin

Ask any students if they know the words to the McDonald's or Subway jingles, and they can almost all perfectly sing them in chorus. In my teaching experience, students love to sing the songs and recite the slogans, as though it makes them feel that they know something important.

Jingles are the easiest way to communicate a message to the subconscious part of the brain, which will retain the information from the advertisement. Slogans and logos have the same purpose of reemphasizing any given product in a way that is easy to remember.

This beginning lesson introduces to students these three concepts, while at the same time explaining how easily captivated we are by different media messages.

Objectives

1. Students will learn how jingles, slogans, and logos are created.
2. Students will reference advertising products and gimmicks they have viewed or heard through television, radio, and magazine advertisements.

Materials

- You will need copies of the advertising terms (Supplement 9A).
- Previously recorded television advertisements, no more than ten minutes.
- An assortment of the most popular products advertised in magazines.
  - Note: Keep in mind that all advertisements should be current and applicable to your audience of students.
- You will need copies of the advertising jingles and slogans. (Supplements 9B and 9D.) You may also wish to create a similar worksheet with a variety of logos.

Process

- Introduce the class to advertisements by showing a five- to ten-minute tape of recorded advertisements.
  - Stop the tape at various points and ask students to name the products they recognize.
- Introduce terms related to this advertising lesson.
  - Jingle—A short song, usually mentioning a brand or product benefit, used in a commercial.
  - Logo—Company or product identifier.

- Slogan—Phrase used to advertise a product or to identify a company or organization.
- Ask students:
    - What attracts you to advertisements?
    - Do you feel that advertisers correctly represent you in their goal to attract you to buy a product?
- Discuss with students how easy it is to recall product names because of jingles, slogans, and logos.
- Chart with students on the board what they consider to be the five most popular:
    - Snack foods
    - Sneaker brands
    - Fast food restaurants
- Ask students:
    - Why did they consider these brands to be the most popular?
    - What makes them popular?
        - Answers will vary, but most will indicate television, radio, or magazine commercials.
- Hand out to students the first slogan and jingle activity sheet found in Supplement 9B.
    - Allow students to work independently for ten minutes.
- Bring the class together again and review the students' ideas.
    - Note: This portion of the lesson will encourage many positive and outspoken volunteers.
- If desired, distribute to students a similar logo activities sheet.
    - Allow students to work independently for five to ten minutes.
- Bring the class together again and review the students' ideas.
    - Note: This portion of the lesson will encourage many positive and outspoken volunteers.
- Close class with a reminder that advertisers spend a lot of time and money to reinforce their products with all consumers on a daily basis.

Assessment

Students will be assessed on their completion and participation in each activity that is conducted during the class period.

Reflection

This lesson is very enjoyable for students. All of the activities presented during the lesson can be accomplished by all students. You will hear many say, "I know that one!" You'll certainly get more students volunteering than ever before, and your main job will be to manage their outspokenness.

The value in this lesson is that while the students feel they are being entertained, they are really learning about consumerism and marketing. More important, students are learning in a very concrete and observable way the media literacy lesson that "all messages are constructed for profit."

LESSON 9.2: DECONSTRUCTING ADS

Before You Begin

Ad deconstruction asks students to evaluate and analyze a variety of ads from all forms of media. While this lesson can be taught with previously taped television advertisements or radio advertisements, the easiest way to lead this lesson is to use magazine ads, because they can be cut out by the student and studied at length.

Food and clothing advertisements are the most prevalent ads targeting teens. Almost any teen-based magazine will carry page after page of popular name brands such as GAP and Nike. There will also be many snack and candy advertisements such as Snickers and Skittles. Any of these advertisements can be analyzed in terms of aesthetic appearance, the product itself, and the message of the advertisement. More important, this lesson will teach students how marketers are in tune with their teen consumers.

Objectives

1. Students will be able to identify messages created by advertisers to appeal to the teenage audience.
2. Students will understand the term *target audience* and comprehend how that term relates to them as consumers.

Materials

- You will need twenty-five to thirty-five precut advertisements from a variety of teen and young adult magazines.

  - Note: Students can be encouraged to bring these from home, and it can be given as a homework assignment.

- You will need copies of the Advertisement Deconstruction handout found in Supplement 9D.

Process

- Begin the lesson by defining to students the term *target audience*.
- Explain that advertisers spend a lot of time and money to find ways to attract people to various advertisements.
- Select an advertisement to share with the class. Use a product that most students would be familiar with.
- Deconstruct with the class the makeup of the advertisement.
- Ask students:

  - What is the ad selling? What is the language of the ad?

  - Whom are advertisers trying to appeal to? Who is their audience? Females or males?

  - What is highlighted in the advertisement?

  - What kinds of appeal are they using? Color? Emotions? Glamour?

  - Are there any stereotypes?

- Introduce the advertising techniques used commonly to sell products:

  - Bandwagon—Everyone is doing it or in this case buying it; "in" with the crowd.

  - Testimonial—A claim by a celebrity or someone of authority that the product is good or good for you.

  - Image advertising—Associating certain styles, people, or places with the product.

  - Weasel—Imply a promise by using words like "usually" or "chances are."

  - Omission—Missing details about the product.

  - Repetition—Endorsement over and over again.

- Scale—Advertising a product as bigger or smaller.
- Association—Pledging adventure, beauty, and quality.
- Name-calling—Using unsavory terms about the competition in order to make the product look better.

- Group students into pairs.
- Distribute ten to twelve advertisements per group.
- Distribute to each group the Advertising Deconstruction guide sheet found in Supplement 9D.
- Close class by having students discuss their findings from the deconstruction assignment.

Assessment

Students will be assessed on the completion of their advertising deconstruction exercise, their group work, collaboration, and participation in the classroom dialogue.

Reflection

Many students understand that advertisers use a variety of techniques to get their attention; however, they are unfamiliar with the terms that define what they are doing. This lesson provides them with knowledge of how advertisers come up with their ideas and why it is so easy to target teens.

LESSON 9.3: MALL AMBLE

Before You Begin

It is important to begin by giving credit to Barry Duncan, author of *Mass Media and Popular Culture* (1996), who originated the first lesson on the use of a mall for media literacy instruction. Duncan called it a "Mall Crawl" and several years ago he took me on this exercise. I later adapted the lessons he taught me to fit my classroom and created an assessment to help my students learn about the importance of the mall as related to media literacy, consumerism, and advertising.

This lesson will require some preplanning in order to complete. Your first job will be to discuss your plans with a manager at your local mall. Most likely you will need to confirm with mall security that you will be in attendance with your students. They will in turn notify shopkeepers that a class will be coming to do a project. It does not mean that all shopkeepers will be open to students coming and asking questions, but it gives them an idea of what will be taking place.

The second discussion that needs to take place has to do with the expectations you have for your students in a mall environment, including that they will not be allowed to shop at all while at the mall. This project, while in a different area, is still a classroom, and that needs to be clearly stated to both students and their parents.

This lesson will also take two class periods and one full day to complete: one class period to prepare students for the research portion of the assignment, one full day at the mall to complete the assignment, and then one class period to review their results.

Objectives

1. Students will understand how marketers use malls to entice consumers to buy.
2. Students will learn how to interview various people in order to acquire information.
3. Students will analyze the overall structure of stores and determine how products are placed within them.

Materials

- You will need to have permission slips for the entire class.
- You will need copies of the Mall Amble guide found in Supplement 9E.
- Construct a series of mock interview questions that will provide students with some practice before the actual assignment. These questions can be random in nature and just for the purpose of practice.

Process

Day One

- Introduce mall field trip.
- Ask students:
    - Why are malls so popular among teens?
        - Possible answers: Shopping, gathering place, accessibility, perception of safety.
    - What stores do they most frequent?

- Make a list on the board for all to see; include restaurants.

- Begin conversation about the structure and appearance of the mall.

  - Answer: Very few clocks, no windows in most locations, palm trees or other plants, play area for younger children, family bathrooms, restaurants, and lighting.

- Ask students:

  - How does the way the mall is structured keep you within the building? Students may need some prompting.

    - Answer: You lose track of time.

  - How is their attention captured while at the mall in order to enter a shop?

    - Answer: Posters, mannequins, colors, window displays, and sale signs.

- Hand out to students their guide for the Mall Amble found in Supplement 9E.

- Review each of the sections with students.

- Assign students a partner to work with for the duration of this project.

  - Tell students that part of their grade will be based on how well they work cooperatively with their teammate.

- Ask students:

  - Have you ever had to interview someone?

    - Answer: Most have not, so this will be a good time to review how to talk to people and other important aspects of interviewing.

- Have students conduct a mock interview with each as a trial run. They can use some of the questions provided in the Mall Amble guide.

- Close class with a reminder that they will need to be prepared to do some investigative work for the following class.

Day Two

- Gather students on bus and review the expectations for their mall visit.

- Remind students to work with their partners.

  - Note: They must stay together during this activity. This is more for safety than any other reason.

- Remind students of the following details found in the guide in Supplement 9E:

  - The layout of the mall—the location of the entrances, directories, greenery, fountains, benches, food areas, restrooms, and telephones.

  - How might the layout influence people's behavior in the mall?

  - How many stores are there?

    - What stores are next to each other?

    - Are stores grouped in a particular way? Offer reasons for the location of the stores.

    - What design elements or other clues communicate to shoppers that a store is a franchise and not a local store?

    - Do most stores try to appeal to a variety of customers or to a specific type of customer? How can you tell? Include examples to support your ideas.

    - How do stores reflect recent popular culture trends and advertising campaigns?

    - Interview shoppers and store clerks to get their opinions of the mall.

- Tell students that they will break for lunch at the mall and then they will have one hour to conduct interviews.

- Close class by asking about their experiences that day while en route back to the school.

Day Three

- Begin class with teacher observations of the mall experience.

- Ask students:

  - What did they learn?

  - What surprised them?

  - Did they have any negative experiences?

    - Note: Some students will find out for the first time that because they are teenagers, many adults will not speak to them. This is a good time to discuss how teens are shown in the media, which is usually very negatively.

- Match student partners with other student partners and allow students to share their experiences.
- Close class by pointing out how their future mall experiences will most likely not be quite the same since this experiment.

Assessment

There is much to assess during these three days, from how students interact with each other to how they interact with the public. Their group work and their ability to share information will be evident once the Mall Amble guide is reviewed. Therefore, the primary vehicle for grading will be the Mall Amble guide, which will be comprehensive and detailed.

Reflection

This activity captivates students. First, they go on a field trip to a location they frequent on a regular basis. Second, they are looking for items of interest to them personally. The mall provides students with an all-encompassing experience that reaches all of their senses. Also, as an educator, this experience is enlightening. You get to see firsthand how the mall attracts the attention of teens and what stores or products students gravitate to the most. There is no question that we can all learn more and more each day about how this one place reaches so many of our students.

LESSON 9.4: TOY ADVERTISEMENTS

Before You Begin

The most popular way to capture the attention of children is with toys. Toys are sold in conjunction with food and clothes and on their own. All of us have toys in our lives. When we are younger, the toys come in a variety of different forms such as dolls, games, trains, balls, stuffed animals, and video games. As we get older, the toys begin to change and get much more expensive.

A few days prior to this lesson, students should be asked to bring a favorite toy of their choice to class in order to evaluate how the advertisers marketed the product to them. This lesson plan looks at toy advertisements from the perspective of the students and their own experiences with the desire to purchase these products.

Objectives

1. Students will identify how toy media messages are constructed in various media.
2. Students will define demographics for a variety of toy advertisements.

Materials

- A class set of Toys "R" Us flyers.
  - Note: Students may also bring their own. You may also want to give this as a homework assignment.
- Computer lab for the whole class with Internet access and a word processing program.
- Digital camera(s).

Process

- Begin class by asking students:
  - Whom are toy advertising companies targeting?
- Introduce students to the following term:
  - Demographics-Statistics based on population factors such as age, gender, and marital status.
- Hand out a Toys "R" Us flyer to each student.
- Group students into pairs.
- Have students look through the flyer and answer the following questions:
  - What kinds of racial backgrounds do the children in the flyer represent?
    - African American?
    - White?
    - Hispanic?
    - Indian? Asian?
  - Look at the price of the toy associated with each child.
    - What is the implication?
  - Look through the pictures of children and estimate the age range of the children.

- Pick a toy that attracts your attention.
  - What is the toy and why did it catch your eye?
- Go to the computer lab and visit the following sites:
  - Consumer Reports for Kids, www.zillions.org
  - CreatAbility Toys: Museum of Advertising Icons, www.toymuseum.com
  - Find a Web site about the toy that you have picked from the flyer.
    - What did you learn about the product?
- Tell students to take out the toys that they brought in from home.
- Have students complete the following directions:
  - Open a word processing program document.
  - Take a digital picture of their toy or find one on-line.
- Insert a picture of your toy into the word processing program.
- Answer the following questions in the word processing program:
  - Name of the toy and what companies make it.
  - When did you get the toy?
  - Did you see an advertisement for the toy and then ask for it? If so, what about the advertisement caught your attention?
  - Why do you or did you like the toy?
  - Were you disappointed with it when you received it or was it exactly what you wanted?
  - Are toy advertisements ever targeted toward parents, or are they always directed at children?
    - Note: You may want to have some more detailed directions for students on the formatting of the paper.
- Close the class with a few presentations from the students' findings.

Assessment

Students will be mainly assessed on the paper that they complete in the computer lab. They will also be evaluated on their classroom collaboration and their participation.

Reflection

This is another lesson that keeps students' attention. Toys are products that are very much a part of their daily lives. This lesson is also personal and geared to their own likes and dislikes. At the same time, it gives them an understanding of how demographics play into what is considered a popular toy for certain groups or individuals.

LESSON 9.5: PHARMACEUTICAL ADS

Before You Begin:

This lesson will require that students watch for pharmaceutical ads during television's prime time from 7 PM to 10 PM for at least three days prior to the actual lesson. This could easily be given as a homework assignment. Have students take notes on the drug's name, the manufacturer, and what it is used to treat. Also, they should note if they see the same commercial more than once. This way, when the discussion takes place, students will have some background knowledge. They should have a collection of ten different pharmaceutical ads.

Objectives

1. Students will understand why prescription drugs are a hot commodity in today's media-filled world.
2. Students will understand the term *disclaimer*.
3. Students will analyze the messages that these ads give to consumers.

Materials

- A TV and VCR or DVD player.
- A tape with ten minutes of pharmaceutical advertisements.
- You will also need enough pharmaceutical magazine advertisements for an entire class. Many of these advertisements can be found in magazines directed to an adult audience, such as *GQ*, *People*, *Vogue*, *Time*, or *Newsweek*.
  - Note: Magazine ads provide much more detailed information about the variety of pharmaceutical ads and their cautionary warnings.

Process

- Begin class by introducing the following term:

    - Pharmaceutical—A medical drug.

- Compile with students a list of pharmaceuticals they are aware of from the media.

    - List them on the board.

        - Answers may include Zoloft, Viagra, Claritin, and Levitra.

- Introduce the following term:

    - Disclaimer—A legal statement, which in this case states that the pharmaceutical drug advertised may have some negative side effects on some people who have taken the drug.

- Ask students:

    - Why are pharmaceutical ads so popular?

        - Answer: Students will provide a variety of answers; however, these ads are so popular because pharmaceutical companies are a billion-dollar business that tripled their bottom line because the FCC allowed them to advertise on television.

    - Whom are these companies targeting?

        - Answer: The companies are targeting mostly adults; however, some products are targeted to children.

    - Why are these ads so effective?

        - Answer: People watch the ads for these drugs and then ask their doctors for a sample or prescription.

- Show the ten-minute clip of collected advertisements.

    - Have students note the different ads seen.

        - What kind of disclaimers are found?

        - Who do they think would buy the product?

- Remind students that these television advertisements are usually about thirty seconds long.

- Ask students:

    - Why do drug commercials carry disclaimers?

        - Answer: Not all products will work for everyone. There is some danger of people getting sicker instead of better.

- Give to each student a pharmaceutical advertisement from a magazine.
- Ask students:
  - What is the difference between the magazine advertisements and the television advertisements?
    - Answer: There is much more information about each product in print than there is on television.
- Have students evaluate the advertisements for the messages the companies are sending.
- Ask students:
  - What techniques are used by these companies to entice people into considering this product for their health issue?
    - Answers will vary, but here are a few examples: allergy medication shows people gardening and smelling flowers. A depression medication will have someone looking sad or alienated by other people.
- Close class by reminding students that these advertisements have appeal because they seek to help people in their illness, and they are personalized in order to grab their attention.

Assessment

Students will be assessed on how well they comprehend the term *disclaimer* and on their participation in the class.

Reflection

This is a lesson that should be done with the older grades (seventh or eighth grade). They are all very aware of the different types of pharmaceuticals sold and whom the companies are targeting. Many students can even tell you what health problem a particular drug may resolve. Also, be aware that some silliness by students may arise when you mention drugs such as Viagra and Levitra.

SUPPLEMENT 9A: ADVERTISING TERMS

Association: Advertising technique pledging adventure, beauty, or quality.

Bandwagon: Advertising technique relating that everyone is doing it or in this case buying it; "in" with the crowd.

Billboard: An outdoor sign or poster found mostly on highways across the United States.

Brand: Name used to distinguish one product from its competitors.

Consumer: A person who purchases and uses goods or services.

Consumer behavior—How people behave when obtaining, using, and disposing of products.

Disclaimer: A legal statement which states, for example, that a pharmaceutical drug advertised may have some negative side effects on some people who have taken the drug.

Image advertising: Advertising technique in which certain styles, people, or places are associated with the product.

Jingle: A short song, usually mentioning a brand or product benefit, used in a commercial.

Logo: Company or product identifier.

Name-calling: Advertising technique in which unpleasant terms are used about the competition in order to make the advertiser's product look better.

Omission: Advertising technique in which details are missing about the product.

Promotion: All forms of media other than advertising that call attention to products and services in order to get consumers to buy.

Puffery: Exaggeration or praise lavished on a product that stops just short of deception. This form of advertising is considered legal.

Repetition: Advertising technique in which a product is endorsed over and over again.

Target audience: A specified audience or demographic group for which an advertising message is designed.

Testimonial: Advertising technique in which a celebrity or someone of authority claims the product is good or good for you.

SUPPLEMENT 9B: SLOGANS AND JINGLES

Name:_____Date:_____

Test your ability to recall the name of the products that match the slogan or jingle.

1. "Obey your thirst" . . . . ._____

2. "Eat fresh" . . . . ._____

3. "Betcha can't eat just one" . . . . ._____

4. "Snap, Crackle, and Pop" . . . . ._____

5. "Don't leave home without it" . . . . ._____

6. "My hotdog has a first name" . . . . ._____

7. "Recommended by Dr. Mom" . . . . ._____

8. "Just Do It!". . . . . ._____

9. "Breakfast of Champions" . . . . ._____

10. "M'm, m'm good" . . . . ._____

11. "Double your pleasure, double your fun" . . . . . ._____

12. "Melt in your mouth, not in your hand" . . . . . . ._____

13. "I'm lovin' it" . . . . ._____

14. "Leave the driving to us" . . . . ._____

15. "Have it your way" . . . . ._____

16. "Think outside the bun" . . . . ._____

17. "Raising the bar"................._____

18. "The first network for men"..............._____

19. "Can you hear me now?"..................._____

20. "It's all inside"................._____

21. "I don't wanna grow up"..................._____

22. "Easy breezy beautiful".................._____

23. "There are some things money can't buy.
For everything else, there's"..............._____

24. "Just 15 minutes can save you 15 percent or more on car
insurance"..............................._____

25. "Leggo my"............................._____

SUPPLEMENT 9C: SLOGANS AND JINGLES—ANSWER KEY

Name:_____Date:_____

Test your ability to recall the name of the products that match the slogan or jingle.

1. "Obey your thirst"........................ Sprite

2. "Eat fresh".............................. Subway

3. "Betcha can't eat just one".................. Lays Potato Chips

4. "Snap, Crackle, and Pop".................. Rice Krispies

5. "Don't leave home without it".............. American Express

6. "My hotdog has a first name"............... Oscar Meyer Wiener

7. "Recommended by Dr. Mom"............... Robitussin

8. "Just Do It!".............................Nike

9. "Breakfast of Champions" . . . . Wheaties

10. "M'm, m'm good" . . . . Campbell's Soup

11. "Double your pleasure, double your fun" . . . . Double Mint Gum

12. "Melt in your mouth, not in your hand" . . . . M&M's

13. "I'm lovin' it" . . . . McDonald's

14. "Leave the driving to us" . . . . Greyhound

15. "Have it your way" . . . . Burger King

16. "Think outside the bun" . . . . Taco Bell

17. "Raising the bar" . . . . Cingular

18. "The first network for men" . . . . Spike TV

19. "Can you hear me now?" . . . . Verizon

20. "It's all inside" . . . . JC Penney

21. "I don't wanna grow up" . . . . Toys "R" Us

22. "Easy breezy beautiful" . . . . Clairol

23. "There are some things money can't buy.
    For everything else, there's" . . . . Master Card

24. "Just 15 minutes can save you 15 percent
    or more on car insurance" . . . . Geico

25. "Leggo my" . . . . Eggo Waffles

SUPPLEMENT 9D: ADVERTISEMENT DECONSTRUCTION

Terms:
Association—Pledging adventure, beauty, or quality.
Bandwagon—Everyone is doing it or in this case buying it; "in" with the crowd.

Image advertising—Certain styles, people, or places are associated with the product.

Name-calling—Using unsavory terms about the competition in order to make the advertiser's product look better.

Omission—Details are missing about the product.

Repetition—Endorse over and over again.

Scale—Advertising a product as bigger or smaller.

Testimonial—A celebrity or someone of authority claims the product is good or good for you.

Weasel—A promise is implied by using words like "usually" or "chances are."

Directions:

Read through the definitions, which have been discussed in class. You are to review a series of advertisements that have been taken from teen and young adult magazines. Evaluate what techniques are used to persuade you, the consumer, to buy into the ad. Check off which technique applies to your advertisement.

Check All That Apply:

1. Name of Advertisement:_____

_____Bandwagon   _____Testimonial   _____Image advertising

_____Weasel   _____Omission   _____Repetition

_____Scale   _____Association   _____Name-calling

2. Name of Advertisement:_____

_____Bandwagon   _____Testimonial   _____Image advertising

_____Weasel   _____Omission   _____Repetition

_____Scale   _____Association   _____Name-calling

3. Name of Advertisement:_____

_____Bandwagon   _____Testimonial   _____Image advertising

_____Weasel   _____Omission   _____Repetition

_____Scale   _____Association   _____Name-calling

4. Name of Advertisement:_____

_____Bandwagon   _____Testimonial   _____Image advertising

_____Weasel   _____Omission   _____Repetition

_____Scale   _____Association   _____Name-calling

5. Name of Advertisement:_____

_____Bandwagon   _____Testimonial   _____Image advertising

_____Weasel   _____Omission   _____Repetition

_____Scale   _____Association   _____Name-calling

6. Name of Advertisement:_____

_____Bandwagon   _____Testimonial   _____Image advertising

_____Weasel   _____Omission   _____Repetition

_____Scale   _____Association   _____Name-calling

7. Name of Advertisement:_____

_____Bandwagon   _____Testimonial   _____Image advertising

_____Weasel   _____Omission   _____Repetition

_____Scale   _____Association   _____Name-calling

8. Name of Advertisement:_____

_____Bandwagon   _____Testimonial   _____Image advertising

_____Weasel   _____Omission   _____Repetition

_____Scale   _____Association   _____Name-calling

9. Name of Advertisement:_____

_____Bandwagon   _____Testimonial   _____Image advertising

_____Weasel   _____Omission   _____Repetition

_____Scale   _____Association   _____Name-calling

10. Name of Advertisement:_____

_____Bandwagon   _____Testimonial   _____Image advertising

_____Weasel   _____Omission   _____Repetition

_____Scale   _____Association   _____Name-calling

11. Name of Advertisement:_____

_____Bandwagon   _____Testimonial   _____Image advertising

_____Weasel   _____Omission   _____Repetition

_____Scale   _____Association   _____Name-calling

12. Name of Advertisement:_____

_____Bandwagon   _____Testimonial   _____Image advertising

_____Weasel   _____Omission   _____Repetition

_____Scale   _____Association   _____Name-calling

SUPPLEMENT 9E: MALL AMBLE

The mall is kind of a wonderland—timeless and enclosed.

Part I.

1. Take a walk through the mall and note how the mall has been set up.

2. Record the layout of the mall—the location of the entrances, directories, greenery, fountains, benches, food areas, restrooms, and telephones. Draw a sketch of what it looks like to you.

3. How might this layout influence people's behavior or perception of being in the mall?

_____

_____

_____

_____

_____

_____

4. How many stores are there? What stores are next to each other? Are stores grouped in a particular way? Offer reasons for the locations of stores.

_____

_____

_____

_____

_____

_____

5. What design elements, logos, or other clues communicate to shoppers that a store is a franchise and not a local store?

_____

_____

_____

_____

_____

6. How do stores try to appeal to a variety of customers or to a specific type of customer? How can you tell? Include examples to support your ideas, such as magazine advertisements, flyers, and so on.

_____

_____

_____

_____

7. How do the stores reflect recent popular culture trends and advertising campaigns? Think of the clothes you wear or the music you listen to and then look at the shop windows. What makes you want to go into that particular store?

_____

_____

_____

_____

Part II.

Go to three different stores and talk to store managers and clerks about their products.

Here are some possible interview questions:

    a. How often do you change displays? Mannequins?

    b. How long have you been working here and what kinds of changes have you seen in the store?

    c. How were Christmas sales?

    d. Who decides when a store is going to have a sale?

    e. Are there any gimmicks that a store uses to entice people to come into their particular store?

    f. THINK OF SOME OF YOUR OWN QUESTIONS TO ASK.

_____

_____

_____

_____

_____

_____

_____

_____

_____

_____

_____

_____

_____

_____

_____

_____

_____

_____

TIME FOR LUNCH

MEET IN THE FOOD COURT

Part III.

On-the-Spot Interviews

You are going to stop and talk to approximately five different shoppers. Some rules of interviewing people:

- Remember to be polite.
- Ask them if they are willing to answer some of your questions.
- Introduce yourself and explain what your project is about.
- Once they agree, ask their first name and then ask your questions.

Possible Questions:

1. **Why do you shop at this mall?**

2. **What stores do you prefer?**

3. **What influences your purchasing? Price? Quality? Other?**

4. **Did any advertisements entice you to come shopping today?**

5. **THINK OF SOME OF YOUR OWN QUESTIONS.**

Name of Shopper:_____

Answers_____

_____

_____

_____

_____

Name of Shopper:_____

Answers_____

_____

_____

_____

_____

Name of Shopper:_____

Answers_____

_____

_____

_____

_____

Name of Shopper:_____

Answers_____

_____

_____

_____

_____

REFERENCES

BOOKS

Cook, Guy. 2001. *The Discourse of Advertising*. New York: Routledge.

Duncan, Barry. 1996. *Mass Media and Popular Culture*. Toronto, Canada: Harcourt-Brace.

Gitlin, Todd. 2001. *Media Unlimited: How the Torrent of Images and Sounds Overwhelms Our Lives.* New York: Metropolitan Books.

Klein, Naomi. 2000. *No Logo: Taking Aim at the Brand Bullies*. New York: Picador.

VIDEOS AND DVDS

Buy Me That! A Kid's Survival Guide to TV Advertising. HBO Production. Public Media Incorporated, 1999.

Buy Me That Too! A Kid's Survival Guide to TV Advertising. HBO Production. Public Media Incorporated, 2000.

WEB SITES

Consumer Reports for Kids
www.zillions.org

CreatAbility Toys: Museum of Advertising Icons
www.toymuseum.com

Don't Buy It! Get Media Smart!
http://pbskids.org/dontbuyit

10 MEDIA PRODUCTION AND OTHER DIGITAL TECHNOLOGIES

> "When people talk to me about the digital divide, I think of it not being so much about who has access to what technology as about who knows how to create and express themselves in the new language of the screen. If students aren't taught the language of sound and images, shouldn't they be considered as illiterate as if they left college without being able to read and write?"
>
> —*George Lucas, filmmaker*

One of the most important ways to teach about media is to produce media. Talking about movies, films, television, and other media environments is valuable, but a hands-on approach to creating media places the student in the role of director, producer, and camera operator; in essence, they become the providers of the media. In this new role, the students are the ones who now need to understand audience and point of view.

By creating their own media productions, students begin to think about how special effects are designed and how difficult they are to replicate. Through trial and error, students learn how to produce scenes that can trick or surprise their audience. The mysteries of any media format are best unraveled when the student participates in the manufacture of his or her programming.

This exercise in learning allows students to see how media messages are constructed based on imagination and understanding. Students take ownership for what their minds can create and express themselves using a video camera, digital camera, or film. All students have the ability to properly use a camera, understand shot composition, and view the images they captured. All they need is an opportunity for instruction and a place to delve into this topic. Without question, they are fascinated with the operation of the machinery, but they are also surprised at how difficult it is to create a quality piece of work.

All the previous lessons in this book have led to this chapter. Chapters 1 through 9 expand on the principles of media literacy through discussion and instruction about messages: dissecting the construction of a variety of media formats, asking students to evaluate and analyze various forms of media messages, and teaching them how to access media information. Here, students are in front of or behind the camera. They write scripts and storyboards and take a concept from an idea to images and film. They are, in essence, the voices and the image makers and the new generation of media makers.

Another important function of production is the collaboration that takes place within groups. Production can only exist when several people work together. Many roles can be delineated within the group, including camera operator, scriptwriter, props, lighting, and talent. One of the first things that need to be done is the grouping. These groups could be formed by the students, but over the years it has become obvious to me that groups decided by the instructors work best. Remind students throughout the production that their assessment will always be based on the work they do as a team. Remind them of the importance of finding a common ground by using the democratic process.

The lessons in this chapter are based upon the theme of media production and can be used with various pieces of technology. Scripting and storyboarding are the outlines of any media program, video production is the tool that designs the work, and editing is the editorial process that happens in our everyday writing lives.

This chapter will provide ideas for how media can be used to develop an original television production using digital video cameras.

Grade Level: These lessons have been primarily used in a classroom environment for grades five through eight, but they are adaptable to all grade levels. You determine what best fits your classroom.

Curriculum Connections:	1. English—Reading, writing, and composition.
	2. Social Studies—Current events.
	3. Science—Ask, investigate, or determine answers to questions derived from curiosity about everyday experiences.
Media Literacy Connections:	1. All media messages are "constructed."
	2. Media messages are constructed using a creative language.
	3. Different people experience the same media message differently.
	4. Media have embedded values, lifestyles and points of view, and omissions.
	5. Most media messages are constructed to gain profit and/or power.
Time Frame:	The introductory lessons for any video production class can be done within two 50-minute periods. One day is devoted to the instruction and the second provides students with an opportunity to practice what they have learned. However, once a production begins, the time frame of classes is determined by the amount of work that needs to be done in order to complete the assignment.

Using the three stages of production, here is an example of how a video production class could be structured:

- Preproduction—If students are producing a newscast, for example, a variety of jobs and topics need to be assigned. Therefore, three or four class periods will be devoted to gathering information and creating a storyboard and script.
- Production—The next two to three class periods would be devoted to videotaping.
- Postproduction—The last two to three class periods might be devoted to editing the materials put on tape or just preparing for the final presentation. If you are unable to edit video, then all you will need is a presentation day for class discussion and analysis.

This is just a sample schedule. Work within the parameters of your own school system and schedule to see what works best for you.

LESSON 10.1: STAGES OF PRODUCTION

Before You Begin

You will need to explain to students different format options. For example, a sitcom is set up completely differently from a newscast; a documentary will look very different from a television advertisement. The exact idea or format that your students will work with is up to you. While you are brainstorming ideas, consider the topic and the students' experiences with the technology.

This lesson, as well as the next four, can be applied to any production that you arrange. The lessons are based upon the three stages of production. Define each stage to students while addressing the expectations for a completed product. You will find that this initial lesson provides an understanding of the process, while at the same time defining the terminology associated with the actual work that students will create. Practice sessions are recommended at each stage in order for students to interact with the equipment and their groups.

Objectives

1. Students will understand the process for organizing a good video production within the three stages.
2. Students will brainstorm concepts related to their production.

3. Students will be introduced to a variety of production terminology.

Materials

- You will need copies of the production terms (Supplement 10A).
- You will need copies of the production stages (Supplement 10B).
- You will need a class set of either lined or blank paper in order for students to brainstorm their ideas, or else students will need to use their notebooks.

Process

- Introduce to students their topic and format for production.
    - This will need to be decided by the instructors, prior to the class starting, unless you feel that your students are capable of selecting this themselves.
- Hand out the list of production terms (Supplement 10A).
- Specifically, define for students the three stages of production.
    - Preproduction—The developmental stage of a film or television program involving scripting, storyboarding, and scheduling.
    - Production—The actual filming of the production.
    - Postproduction—A last stage in the production of a film or a television program, which usually involves editing, adding music, or adding graphs.
- Distribute the Stages of Production (Supplement 10B).
- Review each of the sections.
    - Remind them that each of the sections will become their responsibility.
- Divide students into their production groups.
    - You will know best if students can select their own groups or if it is better for you to do it yourself.
- Distribute to students lined or blank paper for each group or have students take out notebooks.
- Assign students to work in the Preproduction section and brainstorm what they would like to do for their

production. (Refer to Supplement 10H: Ideas for Video Production if students cannot come up with a concept or if you would like to select the project yourself.)

• Close the class by reminding students they will continue working through the check sheet throughout the duration of the project.

Assessment

Assess students on their understanding of the three stages of production. They will also be assessed on how well they work collaboratively within their groups to brainstorm ideas for their future production.

Reflection

It is important to note that production stages that come easily to some students may seem harder to others. There is no question that students love using video cameras and other equipment, but sometimes developing a product is harder than it looks. This lesson defines the three pieces that bring together a fine production. It is important to keep up with students throughout the brainstorming process so that they can be redirected or refocused when necessary.

LESSON 10.2: SCRIPTWRITING

Before You Begin

Consider finding a variety of scripts online or even asking a local news station to provide you with a copy of a script that they have used. In the "Work Cited" area of this chapter you will find books and Web sites that can provide you with additional information.

The most basic way of teaching students about scriptwriting is to compare it to a play. Many students will have seen or read a play in their English classrooms. They will easily be able to translate a theater production to a film production. However, make clear the distinction between a fictional story or theatrical production and a news documentary. While scripts are used for both, the content is much different.

Objectives

1. Students will learn how to formulate a script for any given production.

2. Students will write a script using the following components: setting, characters, dialogue, and identification of props.

Materials

- You will need a class set of the scriptwriting sheets (Supplement 10F).

Process

- Begin class by asking students:
  - Why is it important to write a script?
    - Answers: Students will have a variety of answers. A script communicates to the viewer what the story is about and communicates to the director, editor, and talent what they should be reading and seeing on the screen. The script is a visual representation of what will be seen on camera.
- Ask students:
  - Why might the visual format of a screenplay be important?
    - Answers: Because television and film are visual media and we think of a screenplay as text.
- Ask students:
  - Who is your audience?
    - Answers will vary.
    - The intended audience drives the purpose of the script. Remind students they must be clear about who this is before putting any words on paper.
- Define what a script is to the class.
  - Script—Written document that details the dialogue, action, sound effects, and music of any given production.
- Distribute to the class the scriptwriting example (Supplement 10F).
- Explain to students that the script must include the following:

- • Setting
- • Characters
- • Dialogue
- • Camera shots
- • Sound effects or musical pieces

- Tell students to get into their production groups.
- Assign students to work on developing their production script within their groups.
- Close class with a reminder that scripts must be approved by all group members as well as the instructor.

Assessment

Student will be assessed on their class participation and group work. They will also be evaluated on the completion of their script.

Reflection

Scripts provide the instructor with a clearer understanding of what the students are trying to achieve in their video production. In turn, the students gain by getting their ideas on paper and seeing how they can visually accomplish what they have written. More important, the script gives students the organizational tool for developing their video production. Remind students that greater detail creates a better script for all involved.

LESSON 10.3: STORYBOARDING

Before You Begin

Storyboarding is an essential part of any production because it gives the participants such as the producer and editor a visual look at what they would like to see when filming. For students, storyboarding allows them to think about what is needed in order to actually get the shot on camera. While this is more of a drawing activity than a writing one, students only need to quickly sketch, not become artists. The storyboard must follow along with the script.

Objectives

1. Students will learn how to express the abstract idea of any given production on paper.
2. Students will understand that a visual plan of a production is always necessary before implementation.
3. Students will determine their production needs after sketching the storyboard.

Materials

- You will need a class set of storyboard planning sheet directions and storyboard planning sheet (Supplements 10D and 10E).

  - Note: You should have multiple copies of the blank storyboard available for the class, as students may need a number of sheets in order to complete each scene.

Process

- Begin class by asking students:

  - Have they ever storyboarded?

    - Answer: Many students may have had an opportunity to do this kind of activity in a prior class, and so this will be a refresher.

- Distribute to class the storyboard planning sheet directions (Supplement 10D).
- Review with students what the boxes and lines mean.
- Explain to students that the storyboard must follow a consecutive series of events which match their script.

  - Note: You may want to provide students with an example of a completed storyboard, if you feel it is necessary.

- Distribute to the class the blank storyboard planning sheet (Supplement 10E).
- Tell students to get into their production groups.
- Assign students to review their scripts and begin creating their storyboards.
- Close class with a reminder that storyboards must be approved by all group members as well as instructors.

Assessment

Students will be assessed on their class participation and group work. They will also be evaluated on the completion of their storyboard.

Reflection

In most student production groups, there is a member who likes to draw and wants to work on this portion of the production. While it is fine to have one student be in charge of the storyboard, it is important for all group members to contribute their ideas in its creation. As a side note, storyboarding can be used for PowerPoint design as well as other programs that require some visual understanding.

LESSON 10.4: LIGHTING, SOUND, AND PROPS

Before You Begin

Each of these topics (lighting, sound, and props) can fill a class period, mini-lessons, or as shown here, an overview. Many of us have heard the comments, "Too dark!" and "Too bright!" usually in reference to photography, but the same comments apply to video. If the audience cannot see an image on the screen, they will lose interest very quickly. Sound is another big issue for student productions. Poor sound quality will leave an audience unsatisfied and may turn them off from viewing any material you produced, even if it is worth seeing. The clarity of a narrator or talent's voice is most important for a good production. Lighting and sound both tie in to location, which should be of primary consideration to the student producers. Lastly, a production does not exist without props. A good setting presents the program to the audience, and the clothing must fit the period or topic covered. Students need to understand that these three elements are as important as clarity of image.

Objectives

1. Students will understand the importance of lighting and clear imagery within a production.
2. Students will test sounds and locations in order to find the best place for their video production.
3. Students will create sets and scenery in order to complement their script and storyline.

Materials

- Two or three lighting kits to use as demonstration pieces.
- A class set of the three-point lighting diagram (Supplement 10G).
- A few examples of props to set a scene.

  - An example would be a rainy day. You would need a raincoat, umbrella, and maybe galoshes.
  - Consider having a variety of items available to create different scenes.

    - Note: You may want to consider using these different props as a way of playing a guessing game in which you don't speak but present yourself with your wardrobe. Students would then guess who or what you are trying to imitate.

Process

- Make sure the lighting kits are set up prior to class beginning.
- Begin class by asking:
  What constitutes poor lighting?

  - Answers will vary: Dim areas; place where you cannot see the subject or the scene.

- Ask students:

  - Why does lighting matter in a production?
    - Answers will vary: Emphasize an important point, hide something from the viewer, create mood, and so forth.

- Ask students:

  - How can they ensure good lighting?
    - Answer will vary.

      - A lighting kit is the best way, and many video cameras have a light that attaches to the top.

- Distribute to students the three-point lighting diagram (Supplement 10G).
- Define for students three-point lighting:

  - Key light—This is the main light used on a subject or scene. It is usually placed in the center.

- Fill light—This light is placed on the opposite side of the key light, usually more to the left. Primarily used to fill in the shadows created by the key light. The goal is to soften the image.
- Back light—As the name suggests, this light is placed directly behind the talent or subject and lights from the rear. The purpose of this light is to provide definition, separating the person from the setting.

- Provide students with some time to practice these different forms of lighting.
- Introduce to students the concept of sound.
- Ask students:

  - How does the camera capture sound?
    - Answer: Through the microphone usually found at the top of the camera.

- Ask students:

  - What can interfere with sound?
    - Answers will vary:

      - Noisy room.
      - The subject does not speak clearly.
      - Wind is blowing while filming.
      - Interruptions.

- Tell students that they should wear a head set each time that they are filming and listen to a few minutes of sound prior to a full taping.
- Remind students that the selection of a good location means that the sound quality is prime for videotaping.
- Introduce to students the concept of props.
- Ask students:

  - What is a prop?
    - Answers will vary.
  - Why are props necessary for filming?
    - Answer: They give an authenticity to the film.

- Explain to students that they must be as accurate as possible with props and scenery.
- Tell students to get into their production groups.
- Assign students to review their scripts and discuss with group members the following:

  - Do they need any specific lighting for their scenes?

- Is the location they selected for filming soundproof?
- What kinds of props or scenery are needed for their production?

• Close class with a reminder that class instructors need to approve their final choices.

Assessment

Students will be assessed on their class participation and group work. They will also be evaluated on their understanding of lighting, sound, and props.

Reflection

As mentioned previously, each of these topics can be used as a separate class lesson during which students practice each concept. For the purpose of this lesson, it was important to understand their importance in a general way. During the first filming of any production, it is important for teachers to keep a watchful eye on what is being filmed. Students easily become lost in their stories and forget about the aesthetic elements of filming. Part of your job will be to keep students thinking about these elements through the production.

LESSON 10.5: VIDEO CAMERA USAGE

Before You Begin

This lesson is conducted as a demonstration during which students are able to follow along with the instructor. This requires that each production group have a camera to work with during this timeframe. However, if a camera is not available for each group, then a display system should be made available in which an LCD projector can be hooked up to a video camera and the demonstration can be done in this manner. Most school library media specialists are aware of projection systems that can be best used in either the library or the classroom.

Objectives

1. Students will learn to set up and operate a video camera.
2. Students will understand camera movements and frames.

Materials

- Four or five video cameras, enough for each production group
- Four or five tripods
- Four or five video tapes
- A projection system that allows you to demonstrate use of the video camera
- A class set of the Video Camera Scavenger Hunt (Supplement 10C)

Process

- Begin class by distributing to each production group a video camera, tripods, and video tapes.
- Explain to students the following functions:
  - Removal of the lens cap
  - Installing a battery
  - Inserting a videotape
  - Powering up the camera
  - Using the record function
  - Zoom in and zoom out
  - Setting up a camera on a tripod
  - Checking the viewfinder
- Remind students to pay attention to the viewfinder.
  - Viewfinder—A miniature TV set which allows a person to view the action. Today's mini-cameras allow for a better view because the LCD panel pops out of the camera.
  - The viewfinder lets the camera person know if the battery is going low, if the shot they are seeing is coming in clearly, and more important, if the action is recorded.
- Allow students in their production groups ten minutes to experiment with their video camera.
- Gather the class together again and discuss handling of the camera with the following tips:
  - Do not get "zoom happy." It distracts the audience from the subject.
  - Keep shots steady.

- Hold the shot long enough to record information and see what is happening.
- Focus on your subject matter and do not deviate by wasting tape time.
- Shoot lots of footage. It will help with any editing later.

- Allow students to ask questions at any point during this discussion.
- Introduce the camera movements and shots:

  - Close-up—Head and shoulders shot; when used, indicates the importance of a character.
  - Medium shot—Done usually from the waist up.
  - Wide shot—An establishing shot that gathers in a lot of information; also known as the background shot.
  - Pan—A right or left movement usually done when on the tripod for a steadier shot.
  - Tilt—An up-and-down movement usually done when on the tripod for a steadier shot.
  - Zoom In/Out—A camera lens movement that makes the talent come closer or farther away. Do not use this excessively.
  - Truck—Mostly done when the camera is on a tripod with wheels in which the camera is moved in horizontal direction in sync with the action taking place or following the talent.
  - Dolly—Mostly done when the camera is on a tripod with wheels in which the camera is rolling toward or away from the talent.

- Allow students in their production groups ten to fifteen minutes to experiment with their video camera.
- Distribute to students the Video Camera Scavenger Hunt (Supplement 10C).
- Tell students to work in their production groups and record what is indicated on the Video Camera Scavenger Hunt sheet.
- Remind students that each group member should have an opportunity to use the video camera and participate in the filming.
- Close class with a student showing of the material they recorded and reviewing the new vocabulary words learned.

Assessment

Student will be assessed on their class participation and group work. They will also be evaluated on their use of the video camera.

Reflection

This is usually a very enjoyable class for students and instructors. Students are ready to use the video camera at a moment's notice and it will be apparent from the start that each thinks he or she is an expert at using it. The instructions you provide for this lesson will produce a much stronger presentation from the students. Keep in mind that each production group should be checked regularly to see if it is filming a clear shot. Your suggestions will go a long way to achieving an appealing production.

OTHER PRODUCTION IDEAS

This chapter has been primarily about using the video camera to create a production; however, other digital formats would incorporate many of these lessons. Both scriptwriting and storyboarding are fundamental to the creation of many media projects. Here are some unit or lesson ideas for the future:

- Radio skits—Put students into groups to develop a radio program. This would allow them to learn about sound and sound effects while also incorporating scriptwriting. The history of radio as media can also be introduced.

- Puppet theater—Using the theater as a base of learning about production is always a good place to start. Puppets are attractive to students of all ages. Students can create the puppets and the story or puppets can be purchased and a story is designed around them as characters. This is an opportunity to incorporate lighting, set design, sound, scriptwriting, and storyboarding.

- "All About Me" Web pages—Students are interested in creating Web pages. Fortunately, there are many programs that are easy to use such as Macromedia Dreamweaver. Students would learn about Web design but also how to incorporate various media files including digital photography, audio files, and video. The concept behind "All About Me" is for students to examine what media can be most found in their lives. Students can take a digital picture of their most media-filled environments (for example, a bedroom or a family room) and then analyze what they see. Students will then include audio files that they have developed or incorporate snippets of music.

SUPPLEMENT 10A: VIDEO PRODUCTION TERMS

Characters: The cast of people who are found within the script and who later appear in a production.

Close-up: Camera shot that shows the person in frame from the shoulders up.

Dissolve: The gradual transition from one scene to the next, most often done by using the fade in/out technique.

Dolly shot: A moving shot that uses a camera on a wheeled platform.

Editor: The person often responsible for the outcome of production.

Fade-in/out: Signifies the opening or the closing of a scene.

Jump cut: A cut made in the middle of a continuous shot rather than between shots, which breaks up the continuity of the video shown.

Pan: A horizontal movement of the camera from a predetermined point.

Point of view: The vantage point or outlook from which the action is being filmed.

Postproduction: The last stage in the production of a film or television program, which usually involves editing and adding music or graphs.

Preproduction: The developmental stage of a film or television program involving scripting, storyboarding, scheduling, etc.

Production: The stage in which videos are compiled based on pre-production work of storyboarding and scriptwriting.

Scene: A series of shots taken to show the movie's story.

Script: A written document that details the dialogue, action, sound effects, music, etc. of any given production.

Shot: A unit or piece of unedited film.

Storyboard: A series of sketches drawn in sequence, usually in small, square boxes, which help illustrate the plot and characters in a film, television show, or advertisement.

Voiceover: A voice that comes through when images appear on the screen, but the person speaking is not visible to the audience; also known in many cases as a narrator.

Zoom-in/out: A camera function that allows you to bring your subject matter closer or further away.

SUPPLEMENT 10B: STAGES OF PRODUCTION

The following is a list of what needs to be done in order to have a quality production. Check them off while the production is in progress.

PREPRODUCTION:

☐ Brainstorm the topic for your production for an idea that you and your group can agree on.

☐ Decide on which role each of your group members will take on. Some of these should be done as a group, while others can be done individually. More than one job can be assigned to a group member.

    ○   Talent
    ○   Director
    ○   Editor
    ○   Camera man
    ○   Prop/set design manager
    ○   Scriptwriter
    ○   Storyboarder

☐ Research any background information needed.

☐ Write the script for production.

☐ Design the storyboard.

☐ Gather props needed.

☐ Create the production set.

☐ Practice! Practice! Practice!

PRODUCTION:

☐ Pick a day to tape.

☐ Check on lighting and sound.

☐ Film the show!

POSTPRODUCTION:

☐ Review the tape with the group.

☐ Select any music that you may need to incorporate.

☐ Edit the show.

☐ Present the finished product to the class.

SUPPLEMENT 10C: VIDEO CAMERA SCAVENGER HUNT

Your mission: Find and record ten seconds of each of the following items on a practice tape. Make sure that each member of your group has an opportunity to film these scenes.

1. The introduction of each member of your group on tape.
2. A close-up of someone cutting a piece of paper with scissors.
3. A long shot of a chair.
4. A medium shot of two people standing next to each other.
5. A close-up of a light switch that slowly widens as you zoom out.
6. A shot of someone's eye in the lower left-hand corner of your screen.
7. A long shot of five hands waving.
8. A close-up of someone's earring.
9. A ruler in the right-hand side of your screen.
10. An opened book that takes up the entire screen.
11. A close-up of someone's knee.
12. A long shot of a person that slowly zooms in to show only his or her face.

13. A slow pan of the backs of three people.
14. A creative long shot of any object you wish.
15. A medium shot of any object you wish.
16. A dolly shot of any event taking place.
17. A slow zoom to someone's face.
18. A close-up of a group member, which then pans to another group member.
19. A medium shot of a tree which then zooms in to a leaf.
20. A wide shot of the group.

SUPPLEMENT 10D: STORYBOARD PLANNING SHEET DIRECTIONS

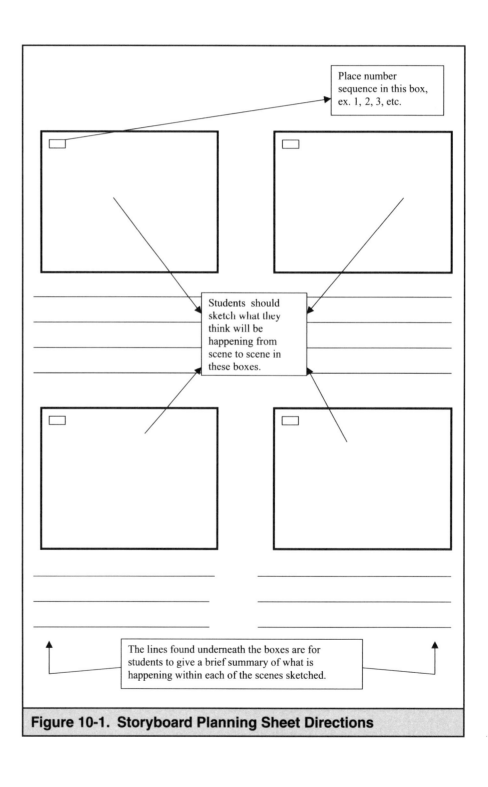

Figure 10-1. Storyboard Planning Sheet Directions

SUPPLEMENT 10E: STORYBOARD PLANNING SHEET

Figure 10-2. Storyboard Planning Sheet

SUPPLEMENT 10F: SCRIPTWRITING

Sample A:

Video	Audio

Sample B:

Scene One: A scene in a script that also has the camera directions.

FADE IN

INT.→At the Office—Daytime

MARK is at his computer typing what looks like an email.

ABBY (O.C.)
(Coming up to Mark's chair from behind.) Didn't you miss me?

MARK
(not looking up)
'Course I did. Why?

No answer. He turns around and looks up:

ABBY
is holding a BOOK tied with a bow.
She smiles. Mark smiles.

CUT TO:

EXT.→MARK'S APARTMENT—MIDAFTERNOON

MARK cuts the ribbon and opens the present while his TWO ROOMMATES watch.

FADE OUT

[end]

SUPPLEMENT 10G: THREE-POINT LIGHTING DIAGRAM

Key Light—This is the main light used on a subject or scene. It is usually placed in the center.

Fill Light—This light is placed on the opposite side of the key light, usually more to the left. It is primarily used to fill in the shadows created by the key light. The goal is to soften the image.

Back Light—As the name suggests, this light is placed directly behind the talent or subject, and lights from the rear. The purpose of this light is to provide definition, separating the person from the setting.

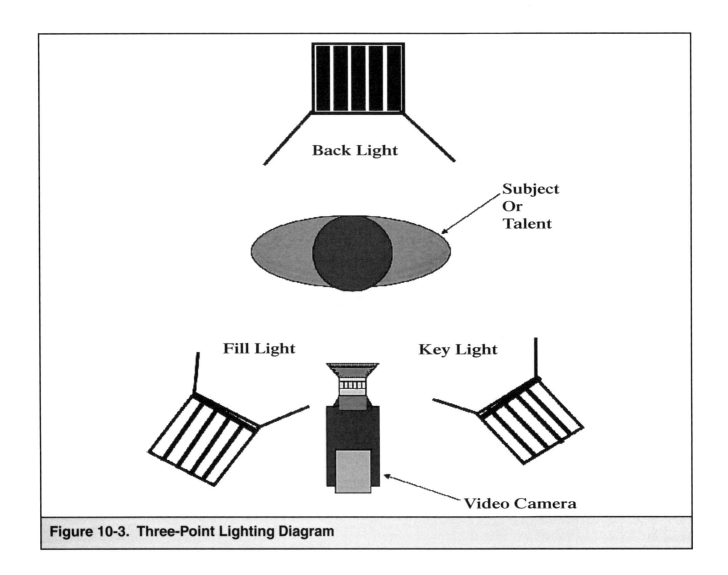

Figure 10-3. Three-Point Lighting Diagram

SUPPLEMENT 10H: IDEAS FOR VIDEO PRODUCTIONS

- Debate an issue live:

  - A presidential debate with class members representing each part
  - An issue that has a pro and con side

    - Too Much Violence on TV: Yes or No?
    - Should Kids Be Allowed to Vote at the Age of Thirteen? Good Idea or Bad?

- News documentaries:

  - Wal-Mart: Profit or Loss to the Community?
  - Gas Prices: How They Affect Our Teen-Age Lives
  - Teen Smoking: Why Is It Still Happening?
  - Steroids: Who Uses Them? Why Are They Available?
  - School Uniforms—Dress Codes: Yes or No?
  - Salaries of Entertainers: Crazy or Not?
  - Controversial Musicians: What's the Controversy?
  - Obesity on the Rise: Causes and Effects
  - First Amendment: Freedom of Speech and Press
  - Youth Sports Pressure: What's It All About?
  - Advertising: Ploys and Gimmicks
  - Music Ratings: Do They Make a Difference?

- Feature Stories

  - A Look at the Cultural Heritage of a Community
  - Focus on:_____

    - A student who has had an impact on his or her peers
    - A disease that students are concerned about
    - A sporting event that has not been covered before
    - An event in the school or town that has people talking

- Clay Animation

  - Clay figures are created and animated on tape.

- The Apprentice for Kids

  - A takeoff on the television show, but with students participating in the projects. Each week a different episode and a different scenario can be presented.

- Public Service Announcement

  - These PSAs can be for a variety of things, such as a health issue or environmental concerns.

- A Class Video Yearbook with a Twist

  - Done as a year in review with commentary on the different events that have taken place throughout the academic year.

REFERENCES

BOOKS

Considine, David, and Gail Hailey. 1992. *Visual Messages Integrating Imagery into Instruction.* Englewood, CO: Teacher Ideas Press.

Kenney, Robert. 2001. *Teaching TV Production in a Digital World.* Westport, CT: Libraries Unlimited.

Rosenkranz, Patrick. 1995. *The Classroom Video Producer's Guidebook.* Portland, ME: J. Weston Walch.

Shulman, Mark, and Hazlitt Krog. 2005. *Attack of the Killer Video Book.* New York: Annick Press.

WEB SITES

Cable in the Classroom
www.ciconline.org

PBS Teacher Source
www.pbs.org/teachersource

11 EMERGING EDUCATIONAL TECHNOLOGIES: THE FUTURE IS NOW

> "I make a basic distinction (one that I think is widening) between education and schooling: people, especially young people, continue to learn—and to adopt new media—but institutions, and those who run them, are much slower to change their ways."
> —*Howard Rheingold, author,* Smart Mobs: The Next Social Revolution

Without question, technology moves faster than education. As part of that change, new forms of communicating are introduced while others go to pasture. Yet, in the past few years, our written and oral language has begun to change with each form of technology introduced into society. "Wiki," "podcasting," "blogs," and "IMing" are all words and programs that have changed the way today's youth create and discuss media with each other. Many of these words have even been nominated by various dictionary publishers as the "word of the year."

What we have now in schools is a split from the "digital native" to the "digital immigrant." A "digital native" in this case would be someone who uses the new technology on a regular basis, follows the trends, and adapts easily. The "digital immigrant" would be the opposite. This would be someone who is unfamiliar with the techno language and may never have used any of the software or participated in any of the current formats of communication but tries to use the technology, while always feeling a bit uncertain of his or her capabilities.

In most cases, the immigrant is the teacher and the students are the natives. While students are at home exploring the different forms of technology, schools are still holding classes in the traditional format of pencil and paper. While students understand the concept of skyping, chatting, and IMing, these terms are unclear and not used in many schools. In essence, this means that education is slow to follow technology that can possibly be valuable to student learning. In fact, as this chapter is being written, the Consumer Expo is taking place in Nevada where Steve Jobs, the founder and CEO of Apple, is announcing the newest innovative gadget: the iPhone, a combination of wireless phone and iPod.

The changes in technology mean schools must seek to become acquainted with the new jargon and introduce those changes as part of the teaching structure. The need for change is becoming more apparent by the articles written in library journals, teaching journals, and other methodology magazines. We are hearing about the possibilities iPods offer to teaching students about communicating, listening, and producing. Students have taken it upon themselves in their free time to create blogs and podcasts.

A blog is an online journal. Blogs are probably the easiest items for teachers to incorporate into their current curriculum areas because blogging is as basic as writing. The difference between blogging and traditional writing is that in blogging the platform for writing is localized on the Internet, where response is immediate. Students can blog as a form of response to a reading assignment or to a question posed by a teacher. The exchange is valuable because while using a different medium, the same level of learning expectations can be used. More important, this form of writing is more in tune with where students' current interests lie.

Blogs can be set up by a teacher or via a district server. There are many locations that offer to educators the opportunity to blog with students without any safety worries. Blogging provides for all students to participate equally in a class setting. This form of writing appears to be a very freeing experience because the writer's thoughts can be posted where others can respond to the writer's messages.

Instant Messaging (IMing) and chatting are interchangeable as terms. IMing has become a natural way of life for students. This is a natural way of writing and speaking for today's youth. As teachers, many of us have found ourselves in the position of reading an assignment including acronyms which you may or may not be familiar with, only to need a student to translate. Obviously, there are appropriate and inappropriate times for such a language to be used, and it is important for students to recognize the difference. As educators, however, we must recognize the importance of this form of communication.

Chatting is basic to middle schoolers and is something they can do concurrently with other assignments. This development in technology has provided for students to be multitaskers, which could explain why teenagers may say they are bored in the classroom. While IMing, students can be doing their homework, listening to their iPods, and even watching television. Some students indicate that they have chatted with upwards of ten different people simultaneously. Yet, in a classroom they cannot stay focused. What does that say to those of us who teach in the classroom?

Wikis are online resources that allow users to add or delete information. Most of us are familiar with the controversial *Wikipedia*, the free online encyclopedia. The site is controversial because the information provided may or may not be accurate. Since the site is an open area where people can add or delete information, this causes some worry as to the veracity of the information provided. Yet, many of today's students begin much of their research in an area such as this one. Educating students on the differences of informational Web sites and how to evaluate their work is very important. A great way to incorporate knowledge of wikis while understanding their value is to have students create their own. In this way, students understand the concept while also understanding how easy it is for information to be erroneous.

Podcasting is another form of technology that is just beginning to take flight in school systems. In a podcast the data are converted so that the information can be streamed via the Internet and downloaded to an MP3 player or iPod. A podcast is an audio media file in which people can subscribe to listen. The name originated from the iPod, which is a bit of a coup for Apple, as the company name has become associated with this top-selling product. An iPod is not necessary for the creation of a podcast, however; one needs just the Internet and a good microphone.

Business and media companies have grabbed hold of this form of reaching audiences because it is quick and easy. Anyone can podcast. There is no need for a studio or any type of professional setup. As a matter of fact, many podcasts are produced with amateur quality. Instead, the point of the podcast is to give voice to the creator for whatever information the creator wishes to contribute to the world. In a school, a podcast can be very beneficial as part of learning about sound and media messages. Lessons on radio can easily be incorporated, and students have the opportunity to learn about audience, scripting, and the quality of a broadcast.

The biggest holdup in education for the use of any of these technologies is time and money. Schools may not have the equipment for using any of these products, although something as basic as an Internet line is all that is needed. Moreover, educators are not equipped with the knowledge of using this equipment and instructing students on use. This is one of those cases where the best model for education is to just jump in and try it. Making mistakes becomes a part of the learning, and the best teachers are the students.

SUPPLEMENT 11A: EMERGING TECHNOLOGY TERMS

Chatting: A term used interchangeably with IMing; a form of communicating done online using a discussion platform.

Digital immigrant: A person who is unfamiliar with many pieces of technology but attempts to learn it while always feeling a bit unsure.

Digital native: A person, in this case most of our youth, who has immersed himself or herself in the language, who uses the new technology on a regular basis, follows the trends, and adapts easily.

IMing: Instant Messaging; a form of electronic online communication which relies on the immediacy of the response between two or more correspondents.

Podcasts: Audio files that are published to the Internet which a user can subscribe to and download to an iPod or MP3 player or stream.

Skype: An Internet phone service; a way for people to talk to each other online.

Wiki: An online resource where anyone can add or delete information.

REFERENCES

BOOKS

Richardson, Will. 2006. *Blogs, Wikis, Podcasts, and Other Powerful Web Tools for Classrooms*. Thousand Oaks, CA: Corwin Press.

ARTICLES

Campbell Gardner. "There Is Something in the Air: Podcasting in Education." *EDUCAUSE,* November/December 2005, 33–46.

Prensky, Mark. 2001. "Digital Native, Digital Immigrants." *On the Horizon*. NCB University Press, Vol. 9, No. 5 (October).

Wallis, Claudia, and Sonja Steptoe. December 18, 2006. "How to Bring Our Schools Out of the 20th Century." *Time*, Vol. 168, No. 25, 51–56.

WEB SITES

Apple Podcasting Lessons
www.apple.com/education/ipod/lessons

Blog for America
www.blogforamerica.com

Blogger
www.blogger.com

Edupoder: Podcasting in Education
www.edupodder.com

Kathy Schrock's The Icing on the Cake Online Tools for Classroom Use
http://kathyschrock.net/cooking/

Skype
www.skype.com

Wikipedia
http://wikipedia.org

TEACHING MEDIA LITERACY: THE RESOURCES

A GLOSSARY

Affiliates: Small, independently run broadcast houses all over the country which are owned by or are attached to a big network; for example, ABC owns hundreds of affiliates all over the country.

Airbrushing: Method of retouching black and white or color photographs where dye is sprayed, under pressure, onto selected areas of the negative or print.

Alternative music: A term that came to be used in the 1980s to describe music that was not a part of the mainstream genres; in most cases it described punk rock. In the 1990s this term began referring to grunge bands.

Association: Advertising technique pledging adventure, beauty, or quality.

Bandwagon: Advertising technique relating that everyone is doing it or in this case buying it; "in" with the crowd.

Billboard: An outdoor sign or poster found mostly on highways across the United States.

Blockbuster: Movie that is a huge financial success, making $100 million or more.

Brand loyalty: Name used to distinguish one product from its competitors.

Camera angles: Various positions of the camera with respect to the subject being photographed, each giving a different viewpoint and perspective.

Characters: The cast of people who are found within the paper script and who later appear in the production.

Cinematographer: The movie photographer responsible for camera technique and lighting during production.

Close-up: Camera shot that shows the person in frame from the shoulders up.

Composition: Visual arrangement of all the elements in a photograph.

Consumer: A person who purchases and uses goods or services.

Consumer behavior: How people behave when obtaining, using, and disposing of products.

Cropping: Omitting parts of an image when making a print or copy negative in order to improve or change the composition of the final image.

Cutaway: A brief shot that interrupts the continuity of the main action of a film, often used to depict related matter or indicate concurrent action.

Director: The person in charge of the overall look of a video or film produced. The director directs the action behind and in front of the camera.

Disclaimer: A legal statement which states, for example, that a pharmaceutical drug advertised may have some negative side effects on some people who have taken the drug.

Dissolve: The gradual transition from one scene to the next, most often done by using the fade in/out technique.

Documentary: A film or video that explores a subject in such a way that the information appears to be factual and accurate.

Dolly shot: A moving shot that uses a camera on a wheeled platform.

Editor: The person often responsible for the outcome of a production.

Ethics: A set of moral principles or values; the principles of conduct governing an individual or a group.

Fade in/out: Signifies the opening to a scene or the closing of a scene.

FCC: Federal Communications Commission, the organization that regulates what is seen or not seen on television and grants licenses.

Footage: Raw, unedited shots that are taken for television or film.

Hip-hop: A form of urban, African American music that came to be popularized during the 1970s; its current association is with dancing as much as a genre of music. Some people claim it is synonymous with rap.

Image advertising: Advertising technique in which certain styles, people, or places are associated with the product.

Information literacy: Critical location, evaluation, and use of information.
   – The set of abilities requiring individuals to recognize when information is needed and to locate, evaluate, and use effectively the needed information (American Library Association).

Jingle: A short song, usually mentioning a brand or product benefit, used in a commercial.

Jump cut: A cut made in the middle of a continuous shot rather than between shots, which breaks up the continuity of the video shown.

Logo: Company or product identifier.

Lyrics: The words of a song.

Media literacy: Emphasizes the following elements: a critical thinking skill that allows audiences to develop independent judgments about media content; an understanding of the process of mass communication; an awareness of the impact of media on the individual and society; the development of strategies with which to discuss and analyze media messages; an awareness of media content as "text" that provides insight into our contemporary culture and ourselves; the cultivation of an enhanced enjoyment, understanding, and appreciation of media content; and in the case of media communicator, the ability to produce effective and responsible media messages (Silverblatt 2001, 120).

- Is concerned with the process of understanding and using the mass media while helping students develop an informed and critical understanding of the nature of the mass media, the techniques used by them, and the impact of these techniques. More specifically, it is education that aims to increase students' understanding and enjoyment of how the media work, how they produce meaning, how they are organized and how they construct reality (Association for Media Literacy—Canada).

- The ability to read, analyze, evaluate and produce communication in a variety of media forms (television, print, radio, computers, etc.) (PBS Kids Web site).

- A twenty-first century approach to education. It provides a framework to access, analyze, evaluate and create messages in a variety of forms—from print to video to the Internet. It builds an understanding of the role of media in society as well as essential skills of inquiry and self-expression necessary for citizens of a democracy (Center for Media Literacy).

Name-calling: Advertising technique in which unpleasant terms are used about the competition in order to make the advertiser's product look better.

Network: A central point of operations that distributes programming to a number of television stations; for example, NBC headquarters distributes programming to many affiliates all over the United States.

Newsworthy: Term used to describe an event that is considered suitably interesting to be reported in a newspaper or the nightly news.

Nielsen rating: A measure of what U.S. audiences are watching on television. One point equals one million households.

Omission: Advertising technique in which details are missing about the product.

Pan: A horizontal movement of the camera from a predetermined point.

Persistence of vision: A visual phenomenon where an image is retained in the eye for a short period of time, creating an illusion of continuous motion in film and video; usually understood to be twenty-four frames per second.

Photo aesthetics: An artistically beautiful or pleasing image, usually composed by a variety of factors including lighting, exposure, and angles.

Photo manipulation: Altering images so that they misrepresent the information presented or in some cases telling a lie through a camera.

Point of view: The vantage point or outlook from where the story is being told, and in this case through the camera lens.

Popular music: The music frequently played on radio stations targeting the teen population; considered a version of rock 'n' roll with lyrics that have more to do with romantic love.

Postproduction: A last stage in the production of a film or a television program, which usually involves editing and adding music or graphs.

Preproduction: The developmental stage of a film or television program involving scripting, storyboarding, scheduling, and so on.

Prime time: Peak television viewing time, most often during the evening hours of 8–11 PM on weekdays.

Producer: The final authority in the electronic media production process. Sometimes the producer is the person who raises the money to produce media products.

Production: The stage in which students are compiling their videos that are based on their preproduction work of storyboarding and scriptwriting.

Promotion: All forms of media other than advertising that call attention to products and services in order to get consumers to buy.

Public television: Known to most of us as PBS; noncommercial television.

Puffery: Exaggeration or praise lavished on a product that stops just short of deception. This form of advertising is considered legal.

Rap: A style of music with components consisting of rhythmic lyrics that are spoken over the backdrop of music beat, scratching, and mixing; formerly known as MCing with an accompaniment of DJing.

Record label: A name brand of a company that specializes in the manufacturing, distributing, and promotion of audio and video recordings; examples of record labels are Virgin/Atlantic and Sony BMG Music Entertainment.

Repetition: Advertising technique in which a product is endorsed over and over again.

Rock 'n' roll: A form of popular music that includes a band consisting of electric guitars, drums, and/or various other instruments. This genre has had a cultural impact on society more than any other form of music.

Scale: Advertising a product as bigger or smaller.

Scene: A series of shots taken to show the movie's story.

Script: Written document that details the dialogue, action, sound effects, music, and other elements of any given production.

Shot: A basic unit or piece of unedited film.

Situation comedy: Also known as a sitcom; normally a thirty-minute comedy in which the characters remain the same but the situations, based on day-to-day living, change.

Slogan: Phrase used to advertise a product or to identify a company or organization.

Sound effects: Sounds used to suggest a story element such as background, time, place, or character. Also used to heighten and intensify action or evoke an emotional response.

Storyboard: A series of sketches drawn in sequence, usually in small, square boxes, which help to illustrate the plot and characters in a film, television show, or advertisement.

Syndication: Supplying materials for reuse; in television, this is a way we are able to see programming that has aired from years ago over and over again.

Target audience: A specified audience or demographic group for which an advertising message is designed.

Teleprompter: A mechanism that scrolls text on a screen, to provide cues for a television anchor or presenter.

Testimonial: Advertising technique in which a celebrity or someone of authority claims the product is good or good for you.

Trademark: Icon, symbol, or brand name used to identify a specific manufacturer, product, or service.

Trailer: A short filmed preview or advertisement for a movie.

Trend: A current style or preference.

Voiceover: A voice that comes through when images appear on the screen, but the person speaking is not visible to the audience; also known in most cases as the narrator of the story.

Weasel: Advertising technique in which a promise is implied by using words like "usually" or "chances are."

Zoom in/out: A function of the camera which allows you to bring your subject matter closer or take it farther away.

B   FICTION RESOURCES

Unfortunately, there are not many fiction books available that include the topic of media literacy or media discernment; therefore, this list is limited, but useful.

Andersen, Kurt. *Turn of the Century*. New York: Random House, 1999.

Anderson, M. T. *Feed*. Cambridge, MA: Candlewick Press, 2002.

Barnes, Julian. *England, England*. New York: Alfred A. Knopf, 1999.

Berenstain, Stan and Jan. *Too Much TV*. New York: Random House, 1984.

Brown, Marc Tolon. *The Bionic Bunny Show*. New York: Little, Brown, 1984.

Byars, Betsy. *The TV Kid*. New York: Viking Press, 1976.

Conford, Ellen. *Nibble, Nibble*. Boston: Little, Brown, 1993.

Cross, Gillian. *New World*. New York: Holiday House, 1994.

DeBoer, Ron. *Returning Light to the Wind*. Waterloo, Ontario: Windmill Press, 1995.

Ellerbee, Linda. *Get Real: Girl Reporter Snags Crush!* New York: HarperCollins, 2000.

Schami, Rafik. *A Hand Full of Stars*. New York: Puffin, 1992.

Tashjian, Janet. *The Gospel According to Larry*. New York: Henry Holt, 2001.

———. *Vote For Larry*. New York: Henry Holt, 2004.

Van Allsburg, Chris. *The Wretched Stone*. New York: Houghton Mifflin, 1991.

Wright, Betty Ren. *The Day Our TV Broke Down*. Milwaukee: Raintree Childrens Books, 1980.

C NONFICTION RESOURCES

Abraham, Philip. *Television and Movies*. New York: Children's Press/Scholastic, 2004.

Brown, Les. *Les Brown's Encyclopedia of Television*. Detroit, MI: Gale Research, 1992.

Brunning, Bob. *Sound Trackers: Rock n' Roll*. New York: Peter Bedrick Books, 1998.

Byman, Jeremy. *Ted Turner: Cable Television Tycoon*. Greensboro, NC: Morgan Reynolds, 1998.

Chambers, Catherine. *Behind Media: Television*. Chicago, IL: Heinemann Library, 2001.

Cooper, Alison. *Media Power?* New York: Franklin Watts, 1997.

Edgar, Kathleen. *Everything You Need to Know About Media Violence*. New York: Rosen Publishing Group, 1998.

Epstein, Dan. *20th Century Pop Culture: The Early Years to 1949*. Philadelphia, PA: Chelsea House Publishers, 2000.

———. *20th Century Pop Culture: The 50s*. Philadelphia, PA: Chelsea House, 2000.

———. *20th Century Pop Culture: The 60s*. Philadelphia, PA: Chelsea House, 2000.

———. *20th Century Pop Culture: The 70s*. Philadelphia, PA: Chelsea House, 2000.

———. *20th Century Pop Culture: The 80s*. Philadelphia, PA: Chelsea House, 2000.

———. *20th Century Pop Culture: The 90s*. Philadelphia, PA: Chelsea House, 2000.

Garner, Joe. *We Interrupt This Broadcast*. Naperville, IL: Sourcebooks, 2000.

Gay, Kathlyn. *Caution! This May Be an Advertisement: A Teen Guide to Advertising*. New York: Franklin Watts, 1992.

Gifford, Clive. *Media and Communications*. New York: DK, 2000.

Gordon, W. Terrence. *McLuhan for Beginners*. New York: Writers and Readers, 1997.

Gourley, Catherine. *Media Wizards: A Behind-the-Scenes-Look at Media Manipulations*. Brookfield, CT: Twenty-First Century Press, 1999.

Graham, Ian, and Richard Morris. *Radio and Television*. Austin, TX: Raintree-Steck Vaughn, 2001.

Graydon, Shari. *Made You Look*. New York: Annick Press, 2003.

Gutherie, Donna. *The Young Producer's Video Book*. Brookfield, CT: Millbrook Press, 1995.

Kane, Sharon. *Literacy and Learning in the Content Areas*. Scottsdale, AZ: Holcomb Hathaway, 2003.

Lackmann, Ron. *The Encyclopedia of American Television: Broadcast Programming Post World War II to 2000*. New York: Facts on File, 2003.

Milton, Bess. *Advertising*. Danbury, CT: Children's Press, 2004.

O'Brien, Lisa. *Lights, Camera, Action!* Toronto, Ontario: Greey de Pencier Books, Inc., 1998.

Otfinoski, Steven. *Oprah Winfrey: Television Star*. Woodbridge, CT: Blackbirch Press, 1993.

Petley, Julian. *The Media: Impact on Our Lives*. Austin, TX: Raintree Steck-Vaughn, 2001.

Platt, Richard. *Film*. New York: Knopf, 1992.

Probert, Ian. *Internet Spy*. New York: Kingfisher, 1996.

Serrian, Michael. *Film*. New York: Crestwood House, 1994.

Vitkus-Weeks, Jessica. *Television*. New York: Crestwood House, 1994.

Wakin, Edward. *How TV Changed America's Mind*. New York: Lothrop, Lee and Shepard, 1996.

Weiss, Ann E. *Who's to Know? Information, the Media, and Public Awareness*. New York: Houghton Mifflin, 1990.

Wordsworth, Louise. *Film and Television*. Austin, TX: Raintree Steck-Vaughn, 1999.

D VIDEO/DVD RESOURCES

Buy Me That! The Kids' Survival Guide to TV Advertising. HBO, 1990, 30 min.

Buy Me That 3! HBO, 1993, 30 min.

Buy Me That, Too! HBO, 1992, 30 min.

Deadly Persuasion: The Advertising of Alcohol and Tobacco. Jean Kilbourne, Media Education Foundation, 2004, 60 min.

Empire of the Air: The Men Who Made Radio. PBS Video, 1991, 116 min.

In the Mix Series—Consumer Smarts. PBS: Castleworks, 2001, 30 min.

In the Mix Series—Media Literacy: Get the News? PBS: Castleworks, 2003, 30 min.

In the Mix Series—Media Literacy: TV: What You Don't See! PBS: Castleworks, 2000, 30 min.

In the Mix Series—Politics: Sifting Thru the Spin. PBS: Castleworks, 2005, 30 min.

In the Mix Series—Self-Image: The Fantasy, The Reality. PBS: Castleworks, 1998, 30min.

Is Seeing Believing? How Can You Tell What Is Real? Newseum, 1997, 22 min.

The Merchants of Cool. Frontline: PBS Video, 2001, 60 min.

Modern Marvels: A Video History of Newspapers. History Channel, 2001, 50 min.

Scanning Television: 51 Short Segments on Topics from Advertising to Terrorism. Face to Face Media, 1818 Grant Street, Vancouver BC Canada V5L 2Y8, 2003.

Sell and Spin: A History of Advertising. History Channel, 1999, 90 min.

She Says: Women in News. PBS Video, 2001, 60 min.

MOVIES ON MEDIA

All the President's Men (director, Alan J. Pakula; 1976).

Almost Famous (director, Cameron Crowe; 2000).

Bowfinger (director, Frank Oz; 1999).

Broadcast News (director and writer, James L. Brooks; 1987).

Citizen Kane (director, Orson Welles; 1941).

Control Room (director, Jehane Noujaim; 2004).

Equilibrium (director, Kurt Wimmer; 2002).

The Front Page (director, Lewis Milestone; 1931).

Good Night and Good Luck (director, George Clooney; 2006).

His Girl Friday (director, Howard Hawks; 1940).

The Insider (director, Michael Mann; 1999).

Max Headroom (directors, Rocky Morton and Annabel Jankel; 1986).

The Muse (director and writer, Albert Brooks; 1999).

Network (director, Sidney Lumet; 1976).

Outfoxed: Rupert Murdoch's War on Journalism (director, Robert Greenwald; 2004).

The Paper (director, Ron Howard; 1994).

Shattered Glass (director, Billy Ray; 2003).

Speechless (director, Dennis Washington; 1994).

Supersize Me (director, Morgan Spurlock; 2004).

The Truman Show (director, Peter Weir; 1998).

Veronica Guerin (director, Joel Schumacher; 2003).

Wag the Dog (director, Barry Levinson; 1997).

F GENERAL PLACES OF INTEREST AND WEB SITES

American Film Institute
www.afi.com
2021 N. Western Avenue
Los Angeles, CA 90027-1657
Tel. 323-856-7600

American Museum of the Moving Image
www.movingimage.us
35th Avenue at 36th Street
Astoria, NY 11106
Tel. 718-784-4520

Children Now
www.childrennow.org
1212 Broadway, 5th Floor
Oakland, CA 94612
Tel. 510-763-2444

Federal Communications Commission
www.fcc.gov
1919 M Street NW
Washington, DC 20554

The First Amendment Center at Vanderbilt University
www.firstamendmentcenter.org
1207 18th Avenue S.
Nashville, TN 37212
Tel. 615-727-1600

The Freedom Forum
www.freedomforum.org
1101 Wilson Boulevard
Arlington, VA 22209
Tel. 703-528-0800

KIDSNET
www.kidsnet.org
2506 Campbell Place
Kensington, MD 20895
Tel. 202-291-1400

Museum of Television & Radio
www.mtr.org
25 W. 52nd Street
New York, NY 10019
Tel. 212-621-6600

MEDIA LITERACY ORGANIZATIONS AND LISTSERVS

ORGANIZATIONS

Action Coalition for Media Education (ACME)
www.acme.org
Offers a biannual conference and a discussion listserv for members. Local chapters have occasional meetings and regional conferences in Northern California; Vermont; St. Louis, Missouri; New York; and New Mexico.

Alliance for Media Literate America (AMLA)
www.amlainfo.org
Sponsors the biannual National Media Education Conference and has a monthly email newsletter for members.

The Association for Media Literacy (AML)
www.aml.ca
A Canadian non-profit organization dedicated to promoting media education. The Web site includes materials and resources for teachers.

Cable in the Classroom
www.ciconline.org
Fosters the use of cable content and technology to expand and enhance learning for children and youth nationwide. The Web site has a number of lesson ideas, video streaming, and information for both teacher and parent.

Center for Media Literacy
www.medialit.org
The Center for Media Literacy provides you with a wide selection of teaching tools, carefully evaluated for their quality and importance to the field.

Fairness and Accuracy in News Reporting (FAIR)
www.fair.org
A news watchdog organization, publishing a bimonthly magazine (*EXTRA!*) dedicated to analysis and commentary of the news.

Just Think Foundation

www.justthink.org

Film, print media, electronic games, and the Internet, Just Think is dedicated to teaching young people media literacy skills for lifelong learning.

Kaiser Family Foundation

www.kff.org

A nonprofit, private operating foundation focusing on the major health care issues facing the nation. The foundation is an independent voice and source of facts and analysis for policymakers, the media, the health care community, and the general public.

Media Awareness Network

www.media-awareness.ca.eng

A Canadian-based Web site for educators, parents, and community leaders. This site includes many of lessons and an extensive portion on Internet issues.

Media Literacy Clearinghouse

www.frankbaker.com

A Web site designed for k-12 educators with a variety of lessons and resources.

National Telemedia Council (NTC)

www.nationaltelemediacouncil.org

The NTC sponsors occasional international videoconferences of media literacy educators, with numerous U.S. downlink sites. More important, it publishes *Telemedium, the Journal of Media Literacy.*

New Mexico Media Literacy Project

www.nmmlp.org

This group provides training and materials in support of media literacy. Their mission is to cultivate critical thinking and activism in media culture.

The Pauline Center for Media Studies

www.daughtersofstpaul.com/mediastudies

Promote media mindfulness/media literacy education in schools and faith communities. They have a number of resources available including a special interest topic of film.

Project Look Sharp

www.ithaca.edu/looksharp

Provides materials, training, and support to help teachers integrate media literacy into their classroom curriculums.

LISTSERVS

ACME (Action Coalition for Media Education)
www.acme.org
There are two forms: a discussion list and one to receive official ACME news only. This listserv has much more of an activist bent to its postings.

The MAGIC Network
www.unicef.org/magic/
The MAGIC Network was set up for professionals and organizations working in the field of children and the media to share information and ideas. It's an offshoot of the outstanding UNICEF Web site MAGIC: Media Activities and Good Ideas by, with and for Children.

Media-L
http://listserv.binghamton.edu/archives/media-l.html
A general media education listserv. Provides information on what other educators are doing in the field of media literacy. Also provides a list of articles taken from newspapers, magazines, and other programs around the country on a daily basis.

Media Literacy Theory and Research
majordomo@scils.rutgers.edu
For media literacy graduate students or those interested in media literacy theory and research. To subscribe to the media literacy theory listserv, send the following message: subscribe mltheory to this address: majordomo@scils.rutgers.edu.

BIBLIOGRAPHY

AAP Committee on Communications. "Children, Adolescents, and Advertising," *Pediatrics*, Vol. 95, No. 2, February 1995, 295–297.
———. "Children, Adolescents, and Television." *Pediatrics*, Vol. 107, No. 2, February 2001, 423–425.
———. "Media Violence," *Pediatrics*, Vol. 95, No. 6, June 1995, 949–951.
Alvermann, Donna, Jennifer Moon, and Margaret Hagwood. *Popular Culture in the Classroom: Teaching Researching Critical Media Literacy*. New York: International Reading Association, 1999.
American Association of School Librarians (AASL). "Information-Literacy Resources, Standards, and a Reaseach Toolbox for Student." *SLMR Online*, 1999. Available at: www.ala.org/aasl (accessed December 2005).
"An American Tragedy." *Time* (cover), June 27, 1994.
Anderson, Yvonne. *Make Your Own Animated Movies*. Boston: Little, Brown, 1991.
Bauder, David. "From Beavis to Britney: 25 Memorable Moments on MTV's 25th Anniversary." New York: Associated Press, July 31, 2006.
Buckingham, David. *Media Education: Literacy, Learning and Contemporary Culture*. Malden, MA: Polity, 2003.
Campbell, Gardner. "There Is Something in the Air: Podcasting in Education." *EDUCAUSE*, November–December 2005, 33–46.
Center for Media Literacy. "Getting Started: Strategies for Introducing Media Literacy in your School or District." 2002–2003. Available at: www.medialit.org/pd_getting_started.html (accessed August 11, 2006).
Christel, Mary T., and Ellen Krueger. *Seeing & Believing: How to Teach Media Literacy in the English Classroom*. New York: Boynton/Cook, 2001.
Considine, David. "Putting the ME in MEdia Literacy." *Middle Ground: The Magazine of Middle Level Education*, 6, October 2002, 15–21.
Considine, David, and Gail Hailey. *Visual Messages Integrating Imagery into Instruction*. Englewood, CO: Libraries Unlimited, 1992.
Cook, Guy. *The Discourse of Advertising*. New York: Routledge, 2001.

Dovey, J. "Reality TV." In G. Creeber (Ed.), *The Television Genre Book*, 134–137. London: British Film Institute, 2001.

Duncan, Barry. *Mass Media and Popular Culture*. Toronto, Canada: Harcourt-Brace Publishers, 1996.

"Five Core Concepts." CML MediaLit Kit. Los Angeles, CA: Center for Media Literacy, 2002.

"Five Key Questions." CML MediaLit Kit. Los Angeles, CA: Center for Media Literacy, 2002.

Gitlin, Todd. *Media Unlimited: How the Torrent of Images and Sounds Overwhelms Our Lives*. New York: Metropolitan Books, 2001.

Goffman, Erving. *Gender Advertisements*. New York: HarperCollins, 1988.

Goldman, Robert. *Reading Ads Socially*. New York: Routledge, 1992.

Kaiser Family Foundation. "Generation M Media in the Lives of 8–18 Year-Old." March 2005.

———. "The Teen Media Juggling Act: The Implications of Media Multitasking Among American Youth." December 2006.

Kenney, Robert. *Teaching TV Production in a Digital World*. Westport, CT: Libraries Unlimited, 2001.

Klein, Naomi. *No Logo: Taking Aim at the Brand Bullies*. New York: Picador, 2001.

McLuhan, Marshall. *Understanding Media: The Extensions of Man*. New York: McGraw-Hill, 1964.

"Media Literacy." PBS Teacher Sources, 1995–2006. Available at: www.pbs.org/teachersource/media_lit/media_lit.shtm (accessed April 26).

Monaco, James. *How to Read a Film*, 3rd Ed. New York: Oxford University Press, 2000.

Myers, Greg. *Ad Worlds: Brands, Media, Audiences*. New York: Oxford University Press, 1999.

Negus, Keith. *Producing Pop: Culture and Conflict in the Popular Music Industry*. New York: E. Arnold, 1992.

Newseum. *Is Seeing Believing*? Washington, DC: Newseum, 1997.

"Nielsen Reports Americans Watch TV at Record Levels." Nielsen Media Research, September 29, 2005. Available at: www.neilsenmedia.com

Partnership for 21st Century Skills. "Learning for the 21st Century: A Report and Mile Guide for 21st Century Skills," 2002.

———. Available at: www.21stcenturyskills.org/2004 (accessed September 23, 2006).

Platt, Richard. *Film*. New York: Dorling Kindersley, 1992.

Potter, James. *Media Literacy*. Thousand Oaks, California: Sage Publications, 2005.

Prensky, Mark. "Digital Native, Digital Immigrants." *On the Horizon*, Vol. 9, No. 5, October 2001.

Richards, Andrea. *Girl Director*. New York: LPC Group, 2001.

Richardson, Will. *Blogs, Wikis, Podcasts, and other Powerful Web Tools for Classrooms*. Thousand Oaks, CA: Corwin Press, 2006.

Rosenkranz, Patrick. *The Classroom Video Producer's Guidebook.* Portland, ME: J. Weston Walch, 1995.

Rubin, Cyma, and Eric Newton. *Capture the Moment: The Pulitzer Prize Photos.* New York: W.W. Norton and Company, 2001.

Rubin, Richard. *Foundations of Library Science and Information Science.* New York: Neal-Schuman, 2004.

Schor, Juliet. *Born to Buy: The Commercialized Child and the New Consumer Culture.* New York: Scribner, 2004.

Serrian, Michael. *Film.* New York: Crestwood House, 1994.

Share, Jeff. "What Media Literacy Is Not." CML MediaLit Kit. Los Angeles, CA: Center for Media Literacy, 2002.

Shulman, Mark, and Hazlitt Krog. *Attack of the Killer Video Book.* New York: Annick Press, 2005.

Silverblatt, Art. *Media Literacy: Keys to Interpreting Media Messages.* Westport, CT: Praeger, 2001.

"Teen Burned Imitating MTV Stunt." New York: The Associated Press, January 29, 2001. Available at: www.associatedpress.com

"Teen Burns Himself Copying 'Jackass' Stunt." Reuters, November 11, 2002. Available at: www.reuters.com

"Trail of Blood." *Newsweek* (cover), June 27, 1994.

Tristani, Gloria. "Wrestling for Our Children's Future." Remarks of FCC Commissioner before the Congress on Television Violence, October 12, 1999. Available at: www.fcc.gov/Speeches/Tristani/spgt916.doc

Turn Off the Violence. "Facts & Quotes," 2005. Available at: www.turnofftheviolence.org/facts&quotes.htm

Wallis, Claudia and Sonja Steptoe. "How to Bring Our Schools Out of the 20th Century." *Time*, Vol. 168, No. 25, December 18, 2006, 51–56.

Wordsworth, Louise. *Film and Television.* Texas: Rainstree Steck-Vaughn, 1999.

INDEX

ABOUT THE AUTHOR

Belinha S. De Abreu is an Auxiliary Assistant Professor at Drexel University. As a School Library Media Specialist at the Walsh Intermediate School in Branford, Connecticut, she specialized in the media literacy education of her middle school students. Currently, Belinha's work in technology focuses on 21st Century New Literacy Skills, which encompasses media, visual, and information literacy. Her goal is to provide students with viable, real-life opportunities for learning in various technological environments. This would in turn encourage students to be creative and conscious learners of technology and media.

Prior to her work in education, Belinha enjoyed a fast-paced career in broadcasting, where she worked for NBC in Providence, Rhode Island. She holds a BA in Communications with a concentration in television production and public relations and an MS in Library Science and Instructional Technology, and she is now pursuing a PhD in Curriculum and Instruction at the University of Connecticut.

She is currently a member of the Media Commission for the National Council of Teachers of English and a member of the Alliance for a Media Literate America.